LIVING
BEYOND YOUR
FEELINGS

LIVING
BEYOND YOUR
FEELINGS

CONTROLLING EMOTIONS SO
THEY DON'T CONTROL YOU

JOYCE MEYER

Faith
Words

New York   Boston   Nashville

Scripture quotations are taken from the Amplified® Bible. Copyright © 1954, 1962, 1965, 1987 by The Lockman Foundation. Used by permission.

FaithWords

Hachette Book Group

1290 Avenue of the Americas

New York, NY 10104

www.faithwords.com

Printed in the United States of America

First trade edition: March 2014

10 9 8 7

FaithWords is a division of Hachette Book Group, Inc.

The FaithWords name and logo are trademarks of Hachette Book Group, Inc.

The publisher is not responsible for websites (or their content) that are not owned by the publisher.

The Library of Congress has cataloged the hardcover edition as follows:

Meyer, Joyce, 1943-

Living beyond your feelings : controlling emotions so they don't control you / Joyce Meyer.—1st ed.

   p. cm.

Summary: "A comprehensive guide to the range of emotions that we feel every day and shows how to manage them—instead of letting them manage you"—Provided by the publisher.

ISBN 978-0-446-53852-7 (regular edition)—ISBN 978-1-4555-0729-0 (large print edition)

1. Christian women—Religious life. 2. Emotions—Religious aspects—Christianity. I. Title.

BV4527.M4385 2011

248.8'43—dc22

2011015387

ISBN 978-1-4555-4911-5 (pbk.)

CONTENTS

PART II

Feelings are much like waves, we can't stop them from coming, but we can choose which one to surf.

Jonatan Mårtensson

INTRODUCTION

It seems to me that we talk about how we feel more than practically anything else. We feel good or bad, happy or sad, excited or discouraged, and a thousand other things. The inventory of the various ways we feel is almost endless. Feelings are ever changing, usually without notification. They don't need our permission to fluctuate; they merely seem to do as they please for no specific reason that we can find. We have all experienced going to bed feeling just fine physically and emotionally, only to wake up the next morning feeling tired and irritable. Why? *Why do I feel this way?* we ask ourselves, and then we usually begin to tell anyone who will listen how we feel. It is interesting to note that we tend to talk a lot more about our negative feelings than we do our positive ones.

If I wake up feeling energetic and excited about the day, I rarely announce it to everyone I come in contact with; however, if I feel tired and discouraged, I want to tell everyone. It has taken me years to learn that talking about how I feel increases the intensity of those feelings. So it seems to me that we should keep quiet about the negative feelings and talk about the positive ones. As you read this book, I am going to ask you to make decisions; perhaps that can be the first decision you make. Write it down and confess it out loud:

Decision and confession: *I am going to talk about my positive feelings so they will increase, and keep quiet about my negative feelings so they lose their strength.*

You can always tell God how you feel and ask for His help and strength, but talking about negative feelings just to be talking does no good at all. The Bible instructs us not to speak with idle (inoperative, nonworking) words (see Matt. 12:36). If negative feelings persist, asking for prayer or seeking advice is a good thing, but once again I want to stress that talking just to be talking is useless.

> In a multitude of words transgression is not lacking, but
> he who restrains his lips is prudent.   *(Proverbs 10:19)*

The main theme of this book is that although feelings can be very strong and demanding, we do not have to let them rule our lives. We can learn to manage our emotions rather than allowing them to manage us. This has been one of the most important biblical truths I have learned in my journey with God. It has also been one that has allowed me to consistently enjoy my life. If we have to wait to see how we feel before we know if we can enjoy the day, then we are giving feelings control over us. But thankfully we have free will and can make decisions that are not based on feelings. If we are willing to make right choices regardless of how we feel, God will always be faithful to give us the strength to do so.

Living the good life that God has made ready for us is based on our being obedient to His way of being and doing. He gives us the strength to do what is right, but we are the ones who must choose it…God won't do it for us. He helps us, but we must participate by choosing right over wrong. We can feel wrong and still choose to do what is right. Nobody can consistently enjoy life until they are willing to do that. For example, I may feel like shutting someone out of my life because they have hurt my feelings or treated me unfairly, but I can choose to pray for them and treat them as Jesus would while I am waiting for Him to vindicate me. If I act according to my feelings, I will do the wrong thing and forfeit peace and joy. But if I choose to do what God has instructed me to do in His Word, I will have God's reward in my life.

Feelings in and of themselves are neither good nor evil. They are just unstable and must be managed. They can be enjoyable and wonderful, but they can also make us miserable and drive us to make choices we eventually regret. Unbridled emotions might be compared to a small child who wants to have and do everything, but does not understand the danger some of those things present. The parent must control the child, or he will surely hurt himself and others. We must parent our emotions. We must train them to serve us so we don't become their slave.

If you are ready to master your emotions, this book is for you. I believe I will be able to help you understand some of your feelings, but understanding

> *If you are ready to master your emotions, this book is for you. I believe I will be able to help you understand some of your feelings, but understanding them is not nearly as important as controlling them.*

them is not nearly as important as controlling them. Make a decision that you will no longer let your feelings control you.

This book could be one of the most important books you ever read. The principles in it agree with God's Word and will put you in a position of authority rather than one of a slave. You can have victory rather than being a victim. You don't have to wait to see how you feel every day before you know how you will act. I believe this book will help you understand yourself better than ever before and also equip you to make decisions that will release God's best into your life.

Decision and confession: *I choose to do what is right no matter how I feel.*

PART I

CHAPTER
1

I Want to Do What Is Right, but I Do What Is Wrong!

We human beings are extremely complex. Our emotions are only one aspect of our being, but they are a very important one. Actually, it has been said that emotions are the Christian's number one enemy because they can easily prevent us from following the will of God. I think emotions have been a mystery for most of us. Frequently, we simply don't know why we feel the way we feel. We let emotions confuse us, and that often leads us to make decisions we later regret.

There may be a lot that we don't understand about ourselves, but thank God we can learn. If you stand in front of the mirror and look at yourself, you see your body, but that is only the outer shell of who you really are. There is a lot that goes on inside us that cannot be seen with the naked eye. We have thoughts, feelings, imaginations, and desires that reside in a much deeper part of us than what we see in the mirror. The Bible refers to that part as "the hidden person of the heart" (1 Pet. 3:4). Have you ever felt that there is a person living inside you who is quite different from the one you present to the world? I think we have all felt that way at times.

We are first and foremost spiritual beings; we have a soul and we live in a body. We should pay more attention to the inner person because when we die, our spirits and souls are the parts of us that will live forever, but our bodies will simply decay.

> Let not yours be the [merely] external adorning with [elaborate] interweaving and knotting of the hair, the wearing of jewelry, or changes of clothes; but let it be the inward adorning and beauty of the hidden person of the heart, with the incorruptible and unfading charm of a gentle and peaceful spirit, which [is not anxious or wrought up, but] is very precious in the sight of God.   (1 Peter 3:3–4)

This Scripture is not implying that it is wrong to fix your hair, wear jewelry, or have nice clothes. It is saying that if we pay excessive attention to how we look and ignore the hidden person of the heart, God is not pleased. It would be far better for us to work with the Holy Spirit to improve our thoughts, emotions, attitudes, imaginations, and consciences. If in the eyes of the world a woman is considered beautiful and well-dressed, but she is filled with anger, unforgiveness, guilt, shame, depression, and negative, hateful thoughts, then she is bankrupt spiritually and unattractive to God.

The War Within

We often feel like a war is going on within us. One part of us (the inner person) wants to do what we know to be right, and another part (the outer person) wants to do what is wrong. The wrong thing can feel right, while the right thing feels wrong. Remember that we cannot judge the moral value of any action by how we feel. Our feelings are unreliable and cannot be trusted to convey truth.

A Christian woman may become emotionally attached to a man other than her husband; she may feel that she could never be happy without him, yet deep inside she knows that leaving her family for the other man would be the wrong thing to do. She doesn't want to hurt anyone. She doesn't want to disappoint family and friends, but her feelings seem overwhelming. She battles with her thoughts and emotions and is in the midst of a terrible, relentless struggle.

She talks herself into doing the right thing, but when she thinks about or sees the man, she once again feels she cannot be happy without him. Part of her wants to do what she knows is right, and part of her wants to do what she feels like doing even though she knows it is wrong. She asks herself and perhaps other people time and again, "Why do I feel this way?" She may wish that she didn't feel the way she does. But then she reasons, *How can this be wrong since it feels so right?* She begins to justify her actions by making excuses and placing blame elsewhere. She says that her husband does not understand her and has never been emotionally available. She is lonely and convinces herself that she married the wrong man. These arguments certainly sound reasonable, but still there is something in her that won't let her go without a fight. The Spirit of God who lives in her spirit is convicting her and trying to convince her to follow wisdom rather than emotions.

The woman is a Christian and has a reasonable knowledge of God's Word. As a believer in Christ she has a renewed spirit; God has given her a new heart and put His Spirit deep within her. In her spirit she knows what is right and wants to do it, but her soul, where her thoughts and emotions reside, has a different idea altogether. It wants what feels good at the moment, not what will produce good results later on.

If a woman has no knowledge of God's Word and no relationship with Him, she may not care if what she wants is right or not, but the Christian is unable to sin and not care. She may choose to sin, but her choice is not due to ignorance. It is due to rebellion and perhaps a lifelong habit of letting her emotions rule. The Bible teaches us that those who are born of God cannot willfully, habitually, and purposely sin, because God's nature abides in them (see 1 John 3:9). They may sin, but they cannot do so comfortably and continually. They are very much aware of their wrong actions, and they are very miserable.

The child of God frequently finds that she wants to do right and wrong at the same time. Her renewed spirit craves holiness and righteousness, but the carnal (fleshly) soul still craves worldly things. Even the apostle Paul describes feeling the same way in Romans chapter 7: "I do not understand my own actions [I am baffled, bewildered]. I do not practice or accomplish what I wish, but I do the very thing that I loathe [which my moral instinct condemns]" (v. 15).

Paul goes on in the same chapter to explain more of what we feel by saying that he has the intention and urge to do what is right, but he fails to carry it out. He fails to practice the good that he desires to do and instead does evil. Thankfully, by the end of the chapter, Paul has realized that only Christ can deliver him from the fleshly action, and as we continue to study his life, we learn that he developed an ability to say no to himself if what he wanted did not agree with God's Word. He learned to lean on God for strength and then use his will to choose what was right no matter how he felt. Paul said that he died daily, which meant that he died to his own fleshly desires in order to glorify God: "I die daily [I face death every day and die to self]" (1 Cor. 15:31).

Christians were regularly persecuted during Paul's life, and he certainly faced the possibility of physical death daily, but he also experienced a soul death as he laid aside his own will in order to live for God. He chose to obey God and walked in the spirit (wisdom) rather than in the soul (flesh). He walked according to what he knew was right, not according to how he felt or what he thought, and he expressed those right decisions as dying to self. I will use the phrase "dying to self" in this book, and although it sounds unpleasant and painful, the truth is that we must die to ourselves if we want to genuinely and truly live the lives God has provided for us through Jesus Christ. When we are willing to live by principle rather than emotion, we are dying to selfishness and will enjoy the abundant life of God. I am sure you've heard the saying "No pain…no gain!" Every good thing in life requires an initial investment (which is usually painful!) before we see the reward.

Exercise is painful, but it produces a reward. Saving money means we need to deny ourselves some of the things we want, but the reward is financial security later in life. Working through difficulties in relationships eventually provides the reward of good companionship. Taking time to study God's Word and learn His character requires discipline, but it brings a great reward.

Learning to understand the difference between soul and spirit is vital if we can ever hope to have any measure of stability and victory in life. We must learn to live out of the new nature God has given us while denying the old nature (flesh) the right to rule.

Dave has told me that he remembers the time when he would drive home from work in the evening thinking, *I wonder what Joyce will be like tonight?* He never knew because I changed frequently. Even if I was in a good mood when he left that morning, there was no guarantee I would still be that way in the evening. Sadly, I didn't know how I would be either until my feelings informed me. I was completely controlled by how I felt, and even worse, I didn't know that I could do anything about it. God's Word says that people perish for a lack of knowledge (see Hosea 4:6; Prov. 29:18), and I know from experience how true that is.

I am writing this book because I believe millions of people live that way and are looking for answers. They want more stability. They want to be able to trust themselves and have other people feel they can depend on them to be stable, but they have never learned that they can manage their emotions rather than letting their emotions manage them.

A New Nature

God's Word teaches us that when we receive Christ as our Savior and Lord, He gives us a new nature (see 2 Cor. 5:17). He gives us His nature. He also gives us a spirit of discipline and self-control, which is vital in allowing us to choose the ways of our new nature. He also gives us a sound mind (see 2 Tim. 1:7), and that means we can think about things properly without being controlled by emotion. The way we once were passes away, and we have all the equipment we need for a brand-new way of behaving. God gives us the ability and offers to help us, but we are not puppets and God will not manipulate us. We must choose spirit over flesh and right over wrong. Our renewed spirits can now control our souls and bodies or, to say it another way, the inner person can control the outer person.

The Bible frequently uses the term "the flesh" when referring to a combination of the body, mind, emotions, and will. The word *flesh* is used synonymously with the word *carnal*. Both come from a word that means meat or animalistic. In other words, if the flesh is not controlled by the spirit, then it can behave quite like a wild animal. Have you ever done something ridiculous in a moment of intense emotion and then said later, "I just can't believe that I behaved that way!"? We've all had times like that. I like dill pickles, but when I was pregnant I could not eat them because I had to stay on a low-sodium diet. I wanted pickles so badly that after I came home from having my baby, I sat down and ate a quart jar of dill pickles. Of course they made me sick, and later I realized doing that was excessive and definitely not wise. The way I went after those pickles was not unlike the way an animal goes after a piece of meat.

Without God's help we have difficulty doing things in moderation. We frequently eat too much, spend too much money, have too much entertainment, and talk too much. We are excessive in our actions because we behave emotionally. We feel like doing a thing and so we do it, without any thought to the end result. After the thing is done and cannot be undone, we regret doing it.

We do not have to live in regret. God gives us His Spirit to enable us to make right and wise choices. He urges us, guides and leads us, but we still have to cast the deciding vote. If you have been casting the wrong vote, all you need to do is change your vote. Forming new habits will require making a decision to not do what you feel like doing unless it agrees with God's will. You will have to say no to yourself quite often, and that is "dying to self."

Please remember that wise choices may well have nothing to do with feelings. You may or may not feel like doing the right thing. *You can feel wrong and still do what is right.*

> *You can feel wrong and still do what is right.*

I can want to do what is right and what is wrong at the same time. It is not always easy to choose to do what is right, but it is easier than choosing the wrong thing and going through the misery I feel afterward. I may feel like pouting and feeling sorry for myself all day if I don't get my way about something, but through Christ I can choose to have a good attitude and trust God to get me whatever He wants me to have at the time.

Dave owned a rare, high-performance car for a number of years, and I tried on numerous occasions to get him to sell it. He steadfastly refused, which at times made me quite angry. He rarely drove the car, but we paid insurance fees and personal property taxes yearly. We even had repair expenses. He said he was willing to sell it, but he wanted quite a bit more money for it than anyone was willing to pay. It cost money to have it just sit in the garage, and it frustrated me terribly. Why would he want a car he rarely ever drove when we could sell it and use the money for something else? Even if we didn't get the price Dave wanted, at least we could stop spending money on it! After about four years of letting it irritate me on and off, I finally prayed and gave the entire situation to God and decided that even if Dave kept the car until we were both dead, it wasn't worth letting the emotion of anger control me.

Another two years went by, and then one night our son Dan called and said, "I think Dad should sell his car. After all, he never drives it." I said, "He won't sell it because he wants more money for it than it's worth, but I would be more than happy to watch you try to talk him into it." I gave the phone to Dave, and within less than a minute he said, "Yes, I agree; let's sell it. After all, I don't drive it much anyway." Amazing! Why wouldn't he listen to *me*? It really wasn't about me. It was about Dave and when he was ready to make the decision to sell his car.

I could have gotten angry because he didn't say yes to me but agreed with our son when he said the same thing I'd been saying for years. But I know that God has timing for everything, and it's usually not our timing. I was angry on and off for several years, but once I gave the situation to God,

I had peace while God convinced Dave to sell the car. Notice that I said *God* convinced Dave. He used my son, but God was behind it. God was actually answering my prayer, but He did it in His own way and timing.

Quite often Christians are carnal. They believe in God and have received Jesus as their Savior, but their whole lives appear to revolve largely around the impulses of emotion. The sooner we learn that feelings are fickle, the better off we are. Feelings are often unreliable and not to be trusted while making final decisions. It is nice if we have feelings to support us when we are taking action, but we can do what is right with or without the fuel of feelings. You may have a habit of following your feelings in order to stay happy and comfortable, but you can also form new habits. Form a habit of enjoying good emotions, but don't let them control you.

I love a statement Watchman Nee made: "As emotion pulsates, the mind becomes deceived and conscience is denied its standard of judgment." Remember the woman who became emotionally attracted to the man who was not her husband? She knew deep inside that her actions were wrong, but her emotions were pulsating, and the devil used her mind (thoughts and reasoning) to deceive her. The voice of her conscience was drowned out by her own soul-driven thoughts and feelings.

Let me state again that wanting to do what is right while wanting to do what is wrong at the same time is not alien to any of us. We all fight the same battles, but I want you to make a decision right now that with God's help you are going to win the war.

Decision and confession: *I follow God's principles, not emotions; therefore, I am a winner in life.*

CHAPTER
2

Why Am I So Emotional?

We all have days when we feel more emotional than other days, and there may be many reasons why. Perhaps you didn't sleep well the night before, or you ate something that lowered your blood sugar or that you were allergic to. The occasional emotional day is something we don't have to be too concerned about. If Dave has a day like that, he never tries to figure it out. He simply says, "This too shall pass."

Sometimes we feel emotional because something upset us the day before and we didn't resolve it. We are often guilty of stuffing things down inside us rather than dealing with them. If you are a person who avoids confrontation, you can have a soul full of unresolved issues that need closure before emotional wholeness will come. I remember a night when I was unable to sleep, which is unusual for me. Finally, around five in the morning, I asked God what was wrong with me. Immediately I recalled a situation from the day before. I had been rude to someone and instead of apologizing to them and asking God to forgive me, I rushed through the situation and on to the next thing I needed to do. Obviously, my wrong conduct was irritating my spirit, even though my conscious mind had buried it. As soon as I asked God to forgive me and made a decision to apologize to the person, I was able to go to sleep.

If you feel unusually sad or as if you are carrying a heavy burden you don't understand, ask God what is wrong before you start assuming things. It is amazing what we can learn by simply asking God for an answer and being willing to face any truth He might reveal about us or our behavior. Sometimes we feel emotional because of something someone has done to us or an unpleasant circumstance in our lives. But at other times we feel that way because of something we did wrong and ignored.

When I kept silence [before I confessed], my bones wasted away through my groaning all the day long. (*Psalm 32:3*)

Facing Issues

If someone has a long history of out-of-balance emotional behavior, they may have many issues they need to face, perhaps even long-standing problems that go as far back as childhood. Jesus gave us the first principle to remember concerning stable emotional health when He said, "You will know the Truth, and the Truth will set you free" (John 8:32).

Without confrontation of painful issues from the past, it

is impossible to go forward with a healthy soul. My father sexually abused me, and once I realized no one was going to help me, I decided that I would survive until I was eighteen and could leave home, which I did. I left and thought the problem was over, but it took another thirteen years to realize that the problem was still in my soul. It was affecting my personality and how I dealt with everyone and everything in my life. I had to begin my journey of healing by being willing to look at the problem inside me rather than blaming all my problems on someone else.

I even had to stop blaming them on my father and all the people who had not helped me. Even though what they did to me or didn't do to help was the source of my problem and the reason why my behavior was emotionally erratic rather than stable, I had to take responsibility for the changes that needed to be made in me. Always remember that blaming does no good, and it does not help you enjoy freedom and wholeness. God wanted to help me, but I had to ask Him to do so and be willing to let the wonderful Holy Spirit walk me through several years of healing. God's Word is the truth that eventually set me free from the pain of my past and gave me emotional stability. I pray that the term "emotional stability" sounds wonderful to you and that you will believe you can have it and be unwilling to do without it.

I eventually learned that hurting people hurt people. And once I realized that my father hurt me because he was sick inside, I was able to forgive him. I learned that what happened to me did not have to define who I was. My past could not control my future unless I allowed it to. I learned that I was filled with shame from the past and was partially blaming myself, but what happened to me was not my fault. Guilt was my constant companion, as well as fear and worry. I suffered from many other soul sicknesses as well, but the point is that each of them had to be faced with God's help, and as they were, healing came in each area.

Picture several different-colored shoestrings tied together in knots, each one representing a different problem in your life. If you handed them to someone and said, "Please untie this mess," it would take awhile because the strings would have to be worked on one at a time. I have a necklace that is made up of several thin chains with crosses hanging off them at different places, and it tends to get very tangled when it is not being worn. Each time I decide to wear it, I have to exercise patience to get it untangled. The Bible says that the promises of God are realized through faith and patience (see Heb. 10:36). You can recover from your past pain, from things that have been done to you and mistakes that you have made, but it will require an investment of time on your part. You can either continue to invest in your misery, or you can begin to invest in your healing! You will invest in something as you live your life, so make sure it is something that will pay dividends you will enjoy.

Thousands of times in my life I asked, "Why do I feel this way?" but I was not doing anything about it. I was merely confused and acted out my feelings rather than trying to get any kind of help. The world is filled with people who do this all the time, and they are trying to interact with one another in relationships that either don't work at all or are very dysfunctional at best.

It is possible to understand some of the reasons why we

feel the way we do, but the most important thing is for us to stop defending our bad behavior. We must surrender all excuses because as long as we use the past to manipulate people and situations, we will never be free from it. I frequently used my past as an excuse for bad behavior, but I had to come to a place where I was willing to confront and deal with past issues properly in order to have change.

One of the ways God taught me to deal with the past was by confessing His promises instead of talking about how I felt. I remember one time standing in front of the mirror and saying something like this out loud: "My parents did not really love me, and they never will simply because they don't know how to. But God does love me, and I do not have to spend my life mourning over something I can't do anything about. I will not waste my life trying to get something from my parents that they will never know how to give me. The fact that they abused me was not my fault. I was a victim, but I will not remain one. I will be healthy emotionally and whole in my soul. God is helping me, and every day I am making progress."

We all have painful issues from the past that we must grapple with. They weren't our fault, and it isn't fair that we should suffer because of other people's behavior. Perhaps you were teased mercilessly as a child and still feel insecure or extra sensitive because of that old pain. Maybe someone you loved left you without explanation. Whatever the source of your pain, God loves you. You don't have to spend your life mourning over something you can't do anything about! God will help you . . . He's waiting to help you.

Don't Get Stuck in a Moment

Your future has no room for your past, and I encourage you not to get stuck in a moment or a time frame in your life that is over. Millions of people miss today because either they refuse to let go of the past or they worry about the future. The things that happened to me or to millions of others in life are unfortunate to say the least. Such abuses are painful and they do affect us, but we can recover. God is a Redeemer and a Restorer. He promises to restore our souls, and He will—if we invite Him in and cooperate with His healing process in our lives.

The Lord is my Shepherd [to feed, guide, and shield me], I shall not lack. He makes me lie down in [fresh, tender] green pastures; He leads me beside the still and restful waters. He refreshes and restores my life (my self); He leads me in the paths of righteousness [uprightness and right standing with Him—not for my earning it, but] for His name's sake.   *(Psalm 23:1–3)*

When this Psalm says that He makes us lie down and leads us beside still and restful waters, it reminds me of our coming to the place where we finally stop running from the past and simply make a decision to face it and receive healing. We spend time with God in His Word and presence, learning that He has offered us a new life, one that is filled with wholeness for our spirits, minds, wills, and emotions. When the soul is healthy and restored, it brings physical health to us too.

Many sicknesses and diseases today are the result of

internal stress. No matter how many doctors we see or how much medicine we take, we may be only dealing with symptoms rather than getting to the root of the problem.

It Just Isn't Fair

Sadly, the world is filled with injustices. People go to prison for things they did not do. One of my uncles spent twenty years in prison for a crime he did not commit. His wife, who did commit the crime, confessed right before she died, and he was released. But sadly, by then he had tuberculosis and lived only a few more years. I remember that my uncle was always a very kind man and seemed to have no bitterness at all about that great injustice. I believe his difficult life, lived with an attitude of forgiveness, gave God more glory than someone who has a great life but is never content. Our suffering does not please God, but when we have a good attitude in the midst of suffering, it does please and glorify Him. Having a good attitude while we are waiting for God to bring justice into our lives makes the waiting time more bearable.

Children die, spouses die, husbands and wives are sometimes unfaithful, and wives are battered. We face issues of homelessness, starvation, natural disasters, and many other unspeakable injustices. But in the midst of it all, Jesus is beautiful and He is a God who brings justice. Life isn't fair, but God is. He heals the brokenhearted

> *Life isn't fair, but God is. He heals the brokenhearted and their wounds and bruises. We may not know why things happen the way they do, but we can know God.*

and their wounds and bruises. We may not know why things happen the way they do, but we can know God. We can know His love, forgiveness, and mercy. When we are sad and emotionally distraught, one of the very simple yet profound things that helps is this: to look at and be thankful for the good things we do have, rather than dwelling on the injustices we've suffered. You might think, *I've heard that a thousand times!* But are you doing it?! Knowledge without action is useless.

Many people are treated unjustly; they do not deserve the pain they experience, but I am so glad that even when I go through ugly, painful things, I do have Jesus in my life to help and strengthen me. Through His guidance we can be burned but not become bitter. When we are hurt we will have emotions about it. We may feel angry, frustrated, discouraged, or depressed, but we do not have to let any of those feelings control us. We can manage our emotions with God's help.

When we are hurting emotionally, it is easy to think we will never recover. But once again, I encourage you not to get stuck in a moment in time. Perhaps you did not have a good start in life, but I promise you that you can have a good finish. Hope will release joy into your life. It is never too late to begin again. Let go of the past and take a step into the good life that God sent His Son, Jesus, to purchase for you.

How Much of My Behavior Is Just My Personality?

People tend to be very different from one another in how they act and respond to particular situations. This has been studied in depth, and four basic personality types have been identified. Some people have a personality that is more emotional than others; this group is called sanguine. Sanguine people are cheerfully optimistic, and they are the life of the party, talkative and passionate. They tend not to be as naturally disciplined and organized as some of the other personality types. They don't merely feel and express excitement; they are passionately excited and enthusiastic, especially about things they enjoy.

The other three personality types are choleric, phlegmatic, and melancholy. While we all possess elements of more than one of these personality types, most people have a dominant type that is prevalent in their personality. No wonder it's hard for all of us different people to try to get along together!

The choleric or type A person is strong in his approach to life. We might say he does everything with a bang! He is definite and emphatic about what he wants. When cholerics make mistakes, they are usually loud mistakes. They make quick decisions, are confident, and are born to lead. They want to control and have a tendency to be bossy. They are goal-oriented and find value in accomplishment. The choleric person can get a lot done in life, but he can also leave a trail of wounded people along the way. Thankfully, God can use our strengths and help us discipline our weaknesses if we give Him control. We can learn to have Spirit-controlled temperaments. In case you have not already realized it, I am a strong choleric.

Dave is mainly phlegmatic. He is more easygoing and not emotional at all. He is very logical, which is not only a trait of his personality type, but a trait that is inherent in most men. Dave is very patient and can wait forever for things to happen. He never worries; he is never tormented by guilt. There are a few things in life, like his golf and football games and not taking vacations in cold places, that he is very definite about, but mostly he is agreeable to whatever I want to do. As he says himself, he is adaptable. It is interesting to note that frequently a choleric marries a phlegmatic. They are opposites, but each has something the other needs.

Then we have the melancholy people. They are creative, talented, and highly organized. They need a plan! They love lists! Some of them tend to be easily depressed and discouraged. They need lots of encouragement, especially about their accomplishments. Quite often a melancholy person will marry a sanguine and the war is on until they learn the art of blending and benefiting from each other's strengths while being long-suffering with the weaknesses.

Choleric people are often irritated by the bubbly sanguine because they have things to accomplish and are very serious about their goals. The sanguine has a goal to enjoy life and have fun. Sanguine people are a bit random and don't do well with schedules. If they made a list at all, they probably would not know where it was if they needed it.

An employee and good friend of mine is a wonderful, bubbly sanguine person. She also happens to be my hairstylist, and when she is doing my hair, in forty-five minutes I find out about all of her neighbors, their pets, sicknesses, and automobiles. I learn about what she saw on the way to work and get a full weather and traffic report. I know how much pollen is in the air. If I ask for a receipt she has, she pulls a wad of stuff out of her purse and begins to rummage through it. Sometimes she finds the receipt; often she doesn't. She talks and talks and laughs, and eventually I tell her I have had enough and she will be quiet for a few minutes—and then she starts all over again. But I love and enjoy her! We are different, but we need each other. She keeps me from being so intense, and I keep her from being dangerously disorganized. She has a phone, but I am surprised when she answers it, while I on the other hand take mine with me to the bathroom.

Being around a sanguine person for too long can get on my nerves, but I am sure that I get on their nerves too. Deep melancholies are a bit difficult for most choleric people too. Their strengths are vital to us, but their need for perfection can be a bit overwhelming.

All the personality types have strengths and weaknesses. As I said, most of us have a blend of personality traits. We have one that is more prominent and a bit of one or more of the others. Out of 40 test points, I am 38 points choleric, 1 point phlegmatic, and 1 point sanguine. My husband is phlegmatic, choleric at times, and also melancholy when it comes to his stuff being kept in order. You just don't want to mess with Dave's stuff. He carries a bag of golf hats when we travel, and if anyone squashes them, we pray for them quickly because you just don't mess with Dave's golf hats. Golf hats are not important to me, but they are important to him. Likewise, there are many things that are important to me that don't matter to him at all. We have learned to respect each other's differences rather than striving to change each other.

Everyone is beautiful in their own way, and thankfully God gives us the ability to get along if we are willing to learn about our differences and show real love to one another.

What's Your Type?

One of the most valuable things in life is to know yourself. If you are sanguine, then just know that you will need to be careful not to let your emotions lead your life.

Don't purchase things emotionally, talk emotionally, eat emotionally, or make serious decisions too quickly. Think about what you are doing before making commitments and crave balance rather than allowing your emotions to control you. Why do you feel the way you feel? It could be your temperament, but don't use it as an excuse to let emotions rule you.

If you are choleric, be cautious that you don't try to control situations and people. If you are melancholy, your mind can give you a lot of trouble because you think a lot and want everything done in a very specific way. If you are phlegmatic, you may need to confront things you would rather ignore, or get up and do some things around the house when you would rather just sit in the chair. All of us need to strive for balance in all things.

I mentioned that personality tests reveal that I have one

point of the sanguine temperament, which means I tend to be more serious and not very humorous, yet when I teach and preach God's Word, people tell me that I am very funny. This proves that as we allow God to control our personalities, we become more balanced. I might have a tendency to be too serious, but God flowing through me makes me funny. I love how God helps us in every weakness if we let Him.

> May He grant you out of the rich treasury of His glory to be strengthened and reinforced with mighty power in the inner man by the [Holy] Spirit [Himself indwelling your innermost being and personality]. *(Ephesians 3:16)*

I have included a list of books on the subject of personalities at the back of this book in case you want to learn more about the basic types and their strengths and weaknesses. Studying in this area has helped me immensely to get along well with and appreciate people of all temperaments.

The apostle Paul stated that he had learned to be all things to all people. I believe we can learn how to give people what they need if we understand them. I also believe we can do better at managing our emotions if we understand ourselves.

Many of the answers to the "why?" questions in life are found in simply understanding more about yourself.

Decision and confession: *Whatever my personality type, I will remember that I am now a new person in Christ.*

CHAPTER
3

Tell Someone How You Feel

We all have an inbred desire to tell someone how we feel, but telling the wrong person only makes our problems worse. Talking excessively about a situation can easily drift into complaining, and that is a sin. Take time to read the upcoming Scriptures and really consider what they are saying:

We must not gratify evil desire and indulge in immorality as some of them did—and twenty-three thousand [suddenly] fell dead in a single day! We should not tempt the Lord [try His patience, become a trial to Him, critically appraise Him, and exploit His goodness] as some of them did—and were killed by poisonous serpents; nor discontentedly complain as some of them did— and were put out of the way entirely by the destroyer (death). (*1 Corinthians 10:8–10*)

These verses would be frightening if we did not remember that we live in the age of grace, and we have the ability to repent and receive forgiveness quickly. But it is interesting to note what a serious problem complaining is considered to be. Why? Because God is infinitely good, and He expects us to remain thankful even in the midst of difficulty of any kind. It may not be easy, but He expects it nonetheless.

In our quest to talk to someone about what is upsetting us, we need to be careful not to move into complaining or to make the mistake of talking to the wrong person. You might ask, Who is the right person? If you really just need to vent in a healthy way and perhaps want a good friend to pray for you, then I suggest choosing a trusted friend, family member, or spiritual leader. Don't repeat ad nauseam how you feel. Just express your feelings and follow up by reminding yourself that God can heal you and resolve your situation.

If your situation is serious and you seem to be at a standstill, consider professional counseling. That kind of talking can be healthy because the counselor will try to help you face repressed issues that may be producing unhealthy emotions in your life. Such issues can be poisonous, and it's necessary to work them out of your system. Then you can go on to the good life God wants you to have. I think some people pay a counselor for years and years just to have someone to talk to. But that is not true counseling. True counseling helps you see and face the truth, and once that occurs then the work of healing can begin.

Talking to a counselor can be a good thing, but never forget that the absolute best person to talk to is God.

I find the Psalms written by David very interesting because he was not reticent about telling God exactly how he felt. But he also followed up by stating that he was trusting God to be faithful to keep His promises. Often David would even remind God of something He had promised in His Word. Let's look at just one passage of Scripture as an example:

How long will You forget me, O Lord? Forever? How long will You hide Your face from me? How long must I lay up cares within me and have sorrow in my heart day after day? How long shall my enemy exalt himself over me?

Consider and answer me, O Lord my God; lighten the eyes [of my faith to behold Your face in the pitchlike darkness], lest I sleep the sleep of death, lest my enemy say, I have prevailed over him, and those that trouble me rejoice when I am shaken.

But I have trusted, leaned on, and been confident in Your mercy and loving-kindness; my heart shall rejoice and be in high spirits in Your salvation. I will sing to the Lord, because He has dealt bountifully with me.   *(Psalm 13:1–6)*

If I paraphrased the above in today's language, it might sound something like this: "God, I am hurting so bad, I feel like I am going to die. How long will You wait before You do something for me? Do You want my enemies to say that they've won? God, I have trusted in You and will continue to do so. Let me see Your face even in the midst of my trouble so I can be encouraged. I feel lousy, God, but I will rejoice and have a good attitude because of Your salvation and Your promises of love and mercy. I will sing to You because You are good."

This one Psalm describes the principle I am presenting in this book. We don't have to deny that our emotions exist, but we must not let them control us. Our emotions don't need to control our decisions. We cannot always change the way we feel, but we can choose what we will do in every situation. We can trust God to level out our emotions while we make right choices.

I believe it was spiritually and even physically healthy for David to express to God how he really felt. It was a way of releasing his negative feelings so they could not harm his inner man while he was waiting for God's deliverance. I've noticed that David frequently said how he felt or what his circumstances were and then he said, "*But* I will trust God. I will praise God, who helps me."

I would never suggest that you stuff your feelings inside and just let them eat away at you. My purpose is not to encourage you to be phony and just pretend that everything is fine while you are seething with anger inside or feel so discouraged that you think you might explode. People who repress pain and never learn to deal with it properly eventually either explode or implode, and neither one is a good choice. We don't want to deny the existence of emotions, but we can deny them the right to rule over us.

My purpose is to get you to express yourself honestly to God or to a person God wants to use, and to get you to express yourself in a godly way. I want to teach you to own your emotions rather than letting them own you.

> *I want to teach you to own your emotions rather than letting them own you.*

Something Stinks

Have you ever opened the refrigerator door to an odor that made you say, "Something in here stinks"? I'm sure most of us have had that experience, and when that happens we know if we don't find what the source of the problem is, it is just going to get worse. Not too long ago, I had coffee with a friend and was surprised to hear some of the things she was saying about her church. She expressed discontent with several things, and she did so in a critical and judgmental manner. I left that day thinking, *Something isn't right in her heart.* I heard jealousy, discontentment, criticism, and bitterness. She was discussing the worship department of the church, and it was obvious to me that she was offended that she had been passed over for the position of worship leader.

I tried to get her to see that her attitude was not good, but she wasn't ready to be sorry for the way she was acting. I know for a fact that she talked to several other people and ended up spreading her critical attitude onto them. I was aware that her attitude stank and would only get worse unless she cleaned it up. Several months later she ended up falling into deep sin. The door for the sin may well have been opened in her life through a wrong attitude toward others.

Her stink became an infection that caused very serious problems.

The whole thing could have been avoided if she had talked to God instead of others. She was not talking to me or anyone else to genuinely get help, she was simply complaining. And we've already seen God's attitude toward that. If she had gone to God as David did, she might have said something like this: "God, I am feeling angry because I was passed over for the position of worship leader. I must admit, Lord, that I feel jealous and I think this was unfair. But I will put my trust in You. True promotion comes from You, and I believe that if You want me in that position, You can surely put me there. While I am waiting for You, I will praise You and support the team that has been selected."

By handling it that way, she could have expressed herself honestly, yet maintained spiritual integrity and righteousness. She could have managed her emotions instead of letting them manage her.

When you feel dog tired at night,
it may be because
you've growled all day long.
Unknown

When you feel dog tired at night, it may be
because you've growled all day long.
Unknown

Sing Away the Blues

I read an interesting story in a book titled *Child of the Jungle*. A missionary and his family lived among the Fayu tribe in New Guinea. The missionary's daughter, Sabine, wrote this:

When we first moved to the Fayu, we wondered whether they knew any songs, since we never heard them singing. This question was answered fairly quickly. We had just returned from Danau Bira, and our things had once again been stolen. As we were cataloguing our losses, we heard singing from the other side of the river. It was Nakire singing in a lovely monotone.

"Ohhhhhhh," he sang. "The Fayu are like birds. Ohhhh, they always take from the same tree. Ohhhh, such bad people. Ohhhh, poor Klausu, poor Doriso. They are so sad and wonder where their stuff is. Ohhh..."

Papa was delighted as it became clear to us that the Fayu simply improvise a song to match their situation. The songs only consist of three notes with which they express whatever they are feeling in the moment. It is not the most sophisticated music, but it is a sound I quickly came to love.

Their use of songs to express themselves may be one of the reasons the Fayu do not seem to suffer from depression or other psychological disorders. Feelings are immediately expressed. There are even times set aside for the release of emotions, for example, the mourning song. When the song of mourning runs its course, the grieving truly is finished, and life resumes as normal.

When a person experienced a traumatic event, he might lie for weeks in his hut, not saying a word but singing for hours at a time. During this period, other clan members would provide him with food. Then one day, he would simply get up with the trauma behind him. Cleansed of pain, he would smilingly resume his everyday tasks.

What if we started making up our own songs? "Ohhhh, I am so miserable because my husband lost his job and I don't know what we are going to do. Ohhhh, I don't understand why my friends are blessed and I seem to always have trouble. Ohhhh, when will my circumstances change? I feel like running away from it all. Ohhhh, yes, I feel like running away."

After hearing me preach this in a seminar, a girl on our staff made up a song about her sinuses. It went something like this: "Ohhhh, I am so tired of my sinuses being stuffed up. I just want to breathe; yes, I want to breathe with ease. It doesn't seem fair that I am allergic to the space I live in. Ohhhh, it just isn't fair."

I am sure you get the point. It might help to sing out your true feelings, but always tell God that you are trusting in Him to make wrong things right.

This is the same principle that David practiced. The Psalms are all songs; they are words set to music. And they were David's way of expressing himself honestly to God. We are encouraged in the Bible to sing unto God a new song (see Psalm 96:1). Perhaps part of those new songs that we make up should be an honest expression of how we feel. In venting our emotions properly, we might avoid lots of psychological problems, the same way the Fayu tribe did.

Our Plastic Society

Do you ever feel that we live in a plastic society? We use plastic cards to make purchases, which provides the illusion that we own what we have purchased and brought home, but the truth is that as long as there is a balance on the plastic credit card, it owns us. Credit cards are easy to use, but when the bills come, we are often amazed that we spent so much and the illusion we had disappears.

We often appear to own what we really don't. Many of us work at jobs we hate simply because they give us titles and a feeling of importance. We can undergo plastic surgery or liposuction, have our hair colored, or wear hair extensions or wigs. With an unlimited budget, we could do just about anything we wanted to alter our appearance. We can put on a plastic smile and tell the world we are fine while inside we are falling apart. It's all an illusion.

When we ask people how they are, the answer is usually "Fine," but the person might actually be freaked out, insecure, neurotic, and erratic. As Christians we often believe that we should feel better than we do, or that it is wrong to feel the way we do, so we hide our feelings from everyone. Sometimes we try to hide the way we really feel from our own selves. We pretend to have faith while we're full of doubt. We pretend to be happy while we are miserable; and we pretend to be in control and have it all together, but at home behind closed doors, we are totally different people. We don't want to admit that we are living phony lives so we stay busy enough that we never have to deal with things as they really are. We may even bury ourselves in church work or spiritual activity as a way of hiding from God. He is trying to show us truth, but we would rather work for Him than listen to Him.

God just wants us to be honest and real. Don't fall into the trap of thinking all your feelings are wrong. Being a person of faith does not mean you will never have negative or ungodly feelings. We will experience feelings that need to be dealt with, but we can always exercise our faith in God and ask Him to help us not to allow our feelings to control us. The Bible says we live by faith and not by sight (see 2 Cor. 5:7). That means we don't make decisions based on what we see or feel, but according to our faith in God and His promises to us. I don't think what we feel is a sin as long as we are talking to God about it and securing His strength to choose to act on His Word and not on how we feel. The Bible says to be angry and sin not. That literally means you can feel angry about an injustice, but if you deal with it properly then it will not become sin (see Eph. 4:26).

The truth makes us free. We are to deal truly, live truly, and above all be truthful with God and ourselves. The Bible also says that we are to reject all falsity; be done with it and let everyone express truth with his neighbor (see Eph. 4:25). I don't think that means we should spill our guts to everyone we meet about everything we feel and have done in life, but we cannot have plastic relationships that are built on pretense.

Decision and confession: *I will be authentic and truthful in my walk with God and my fellow human beings.*

CHAPTER
4

Our Secrets Make Us Sick

I recall a time when I had worked so hard for such a long period, and had been around so many people all wanting a piece of me, that I drove by my own office headquarters and stuck my tongue out at it. At that point I didn't even want to hear the name Joyce Meyer. I wanted to go grocery shopping and bake a cake or sweep a floor. I wanted to do anything that would give me a feeling of being just a person. I had let myself get out of balance by trying to "be there" for people too much, and I was deteriorating emotionally from the stress. But after a time of rest and a change of pace, I was whole and ready to go to work again.

I think a lot of people, and especially those in the public eye, can easily develop a habit of living a double life. They try to be what everyone wants them to be and yet deep inside they want privacy and the freedom to just be themselves. The truth is that they want both. They love what they are doing; they are born to lead or act or sing or teach, but they need balance. If they deny their own needs and live just to please other people, they will eventually become dysfunctional in some way.

I love people. I love to be with them and be there for them. But no matter how much we enjoy what we do, from time to time we need a break and a change of pace. One of the reasons we feel unhappy or upset at times is simply because we are driven by a need to please everyone and be accepted by them. We should not let people manipulate us. We cannot let their expectations control us. It is amazing how much we fear being totally honest with people. Even when I decided to share my little story about sticking my tongue out at my own office headquarters, I found myself wondering if I could be that honest and not disappoint people. I decided to believe that my readers are mature enough to realize that although I truly love what I do, there are times when I get tired and just plain want to relax and have time to myself.

One of my children had a particularly difficult time being the PK (preacher's kid). I asked him when he was older what the most difficult thing was for him, and after giving it some serious thought, he said, "People's expectations." He told me that people always expected that he should not be a normal kid who made mistakes like any other kid. They expected more because he was my son. If he talked out in class, a teacher might say, "I would expect more of Joyce Meyer's son." How foolish that teacher was to put that kind of pressure on him. Even though he was my son, he still had to grow up and learn just as any other child would.

People's expectations can often be extremely unrealistic, and if we allow them to, they will pressure us terribly. Don't develop a plastic life and be filled with secrets that are making you sick just to meet people's expectations. Live honestly and truly, and God will give you the right friends who will encourage you to be real and genuine.

In an effort to be honest, a woman once said to me, "I just felt I needed to come clean and tell you that I have not liked you for years, and I have gossiped about you and would like you to forgive me." I forgave her, but what she did was foolish. She cleansed her conscience at the expense of dumping her problem on me. Now I had to deal with it and resist wondering why she didn't like me, what she had said about me, and to whom she had spoken. That is not the kind of honesty God is talking about. There are some things that we should keep to ourselves out of wisdom. We do want to live truly, but the Bible does tell us to speak the truth in love. I've often wondered what kind of love made her share her secret with me.

There are some things you should keep between you and God, but some things must be brought out into the open. I know a Christian man who had an affair with another woman. When he decided that he didn't want to leave his wife for the woman, he also decided that he was not going to tell his wife about the affair. His wife had known for quite some time that something was wrong and had even asked him repeatedly if he was seeing another woman. There was no way they could build a healthy relationship on lies. I told him that he had to be totally honest with her and pray that she would find the grace to forgive him and try to rebuild the marriage.

If he tried to go forward imbedded in deception, he would likely end up doing the same thing again. What we hide still has authority over us and creates fear. His problem still had to be dealt with. He needed counseling to find out why he had been unfaithful to his wife. The man could not ignore the situation and deal with it at the same time. That was a secret that would have made him and his marriage sick.

I have an example from my own life that may be helpful. When I was twenty years old, and that has been a long time ago, I stole money from a company I worked for. The man I was married to at the time was a petty thief, and he convinced me to write some payroll checks since I was the payroll clerk, and we would cash them and quickly get out of town. I am not blaming him because I should have said no, but there are times in life when we let people we love talk us into things that go against our consciences. When we do, it always ends up bad.

We did cash the checks and leave town, but eventually we came back, and sure enough there was an ongoing investigation about the stolen money. I was questioned, told more lies, and escaped being accused of the crime. My husband cheated on me with other women, stole property, and eventually was arrested and went to prison. We got a divorce and many years later, married to someone else and about to enter the ministry, I knew that I had to go to the company I'd stolen from, admit my theft, and pay back the money. Wow! What if they had me arrested? I was so frightened, but I knew I had to obey God. I could not go forward until that thing from my past was confronted.

I went to the company and explained what I had done and that I was now a Christian and wanted to ask their forgiveness and pay back the money. They graciously let me do so, and I was set free from the nagging fear that someday I might get caught. I am convinced that if I had not obeyed God, I would not be in ministry today. God is willing to forgive us for anything, but we must confess it and make restitution wherever possible.

If God tells you to bring something out into the open or confront a situation from your past, be obedient to Him. He is letting you know this issue is holding you back from His best for you.

> *If God tells you to bring something out into the open or confront a situation from your past, be obedient to Him. He is letting you know this issue is holding you back from His best for you.*

Always pray about when and how to confront things, especially things that have been buried a long time. Remember, emotional stability comes through learning to live truthfully.

Perhaps after reading this, you feel that something hidden inside you is poisoning your life and you want to confront it but are not sure if it would be best for everyone concerned. I suggest that you first pray, and if you are still not clear on what action to take, speak to a spiritual leader whom you trust or a counselor to get some advice. As I mentioned earlier, we always want to speak the truth in love, and we want our sharing to bring closure, not create more wounds.

Don't You Dare Tell

It would be amazing to know how many people in our society are mentally, physically, or emotionally sick from carrying around secrets buried inside that are eating away at them like a cancer. If you are one of those people, please start talking to God, and either He will completely relieve your burden or He will lead you in what to do next. It is danger-ous to merely ignore things that need to be dealt with. God's will for all of us is wholeness. It is not living with our souls full of holes and watching our lives leak out day after day. Bringing hidden things out into the open is admittedly dif-ficult at times, but it is much more difficult to keep them hid-den and live in the fear of being discovered. You might need to talk to a trusted spiritual leader, a loving family member or friend, or a counselor. God will direct your steps if you will go to Him and tell Him you are fully willing to stop let-ting secrets make you sick. Having an intimate relationship with God means that you can and should talk to Him openly and honestly about anything and everything. The more you talk to God, the better off you are.

During the years I was being abused, I talked to God. Even though it was in my own childish way and not very polished, the point was that I could not talk to anyone else. But I did talk to God, and I believe it got me through those difficult years.

One reason we find it so difficult to share our secrets is that it is often hard to find someone to talk to whom we can trust. We can't control what others do, but we can learn to be a faithful friend. If someone tells you something in confi-dence, never tell anyone else. If they tell you something that shocks or surprises you, do your best not to act shocked or surprised and don't judge them. The purpose for bringing things out into the open is for restoration, not for criticism and judging.

Brethren, if any person is overtaken in misconduct or sin of any sort, you who are spiritual [who are responsive to and controlled by the Spirit] should set him right and restore and reinstate him, without any sense of superiority and with all gentleness, keeping an attentive eye on yourself, lest you should be tempted also. Bear (endure, carry) one another's burdens and troublesome moral faults, and in this way fulfill and observe perfectly the law of Christ.   *(Galatians 6:1–2)*

The law of Christ is love. If all things are done in love, then they are always handled properly. God is long-suffering and patient, and we should strive to be the way He is. We should always treat people who come to us to share their secrets as we would want to be treated.

People with Secrets

Margaret had a child at the age of fifteen, and her parents forced her to give the baby up for adoption. It was not her choice, but her family convinced her it was the best thing for all concerned. Margaret grew up, got married, and had four more children. She never told anyone about the baby girl she had given away when she was fifteen. The years went by and adoption laws changed, allowing adopted children to contact their birth parents. One day Margaret was home alone and her doorbell rang. She opened the door to a beautiful young lady who said she was her daughter. Joy and fear hit Margaret at the same time. She reacted emotionally, and without really even thinking about what she was doing, she told the young lady that she was mistaken and asked her to never come back. The girl went away sad and brokenhearted, feeling even more rejected than before.

Over the next two months, Margaret became more and more miserable as each day went by. Margaret had a variety of health problems through the years and the doctor always told her it was stress, but she never connected the dots between the secret and the stress. She was now having excruciating headaches and insomnia. Her family realized that something was wrong and continued to press her for an answer. Finally Margaret felt like she would die if she didn't tell the truth, so she told her husband and children about the baby girl. To her surprise they were not angry. Their only disappointment was that she had never trusted in their love for her enough to tell them. The children regretted that they had a sister they had never seen and wanted to meet her.

Margaret had kept a secret for many years that was not necessary to keep. She was convinced that her family would reject her if they knew the truth, but she discovered that they loved her enough to accept her imperfection. They searched for and found the baby girl who was now a woman named Meredith. Thankfully, she had been adopted and raised by parents who loved her very much. Meredith felt that God had been leading her to find her birth mother and although some emotional healing was needed, they all recovered and both families became friends. It is amazing what God can do if we will be honest and trust Him.

During the years I was being sexually abused by my father, he always stressed that it had to be a secret. It was definitely a secret, and it ended up making me mentally and emotionally sick. He said that if I told people, they would not believe me and I would just cause trouble for everyone. He assured me there was nothing wrong with what he was doing, but that people just wouldn't understand. I had not yet learned that if we have to hide something, it usually means something is wrong with it. Many, many years later when I finally did confront my father, he tried to tell me that he did not know what he was doing was wrong and had no idea it was hurting me. But it was obvious to me that if he had not known it was wrong, he wouldn't have told me to keep it a secret.

My mother knew what my father was doing but did not confront it, and the secret made her sick. After years of hiding from the truth because she was afraid of the scandal, she had a nervous breakdown and had to take shock treatments for two years. Her nerves were damaged from the trauma of keeping the secret so many years, and she has taken anxiety medicine ever since. Her fear forced her to keep a secret that made her sick.

I did not tell anyone my secret until I was nearly twenty-three years old, and I remember shaking violently each time I tried to talk about it. It was buried so deeply in me that it was hard to bring it out into the open. I was terribly afraid of what people would think of me. I found most people to be very compassionate. My husband was wonderful, and in later years as I told my children, they of course were wonderful too. I have met women as old as eighty who were sexually abused and never told anyone. How sad for them that they did not know the value of telling the truth. I am sure most of them existed with dysfunctional personalities and had fear as their constant companion.

Sally was a prostitute for seven years, and during that time she had three abortions. It was a lifestyle she sort of fell into after becoming involved in the drug culture as a teenager. She eventually got away from it and tried to do life right, but she seemed to fail at everything. She was married and divorced three times by the time she was forty. She had two children, but their fathers had custody of them because Sally kept going back to drugs and alcohol. She really wanted to get well, but she kept her secrets. Eventually, she had a complete mental and physical collapse, and while she was in the hospital she met a wonderful Christian nurse who led her into a relationship with God. Once she realized that God loved her and had forgiven her sins, she was able to bring her secrets of prostitution and abortion out into the open. The people she had hurt along the way were not as willing to forgive as she had hoped, but she was able eventually to begin a new life and build a new family. She continues to trust God for healing between her and her other two children.

———

These stories show us that secrets open the door to fear and worry. I want you to know that you do not have to live with secrets that allow negative emotions to control you. Our feelings are real and they are powerful, but they are not more powerful than God and truth. Anyone can have emotional wholeness if they learn the principles in this book and put them into action in their lives. Always remember that the truth will make you free.

> Our feelings are real and they are powerful, but they are not more powerful than God and truth.

Decision and confession: *The truth will make me free.*

CHAPTER
5

I Wish I Didn't Feel This Way

We have all said many times in life, "I wish I didn't feel this way." If we could just get what we want by wishing, life would really be easy, but it doesn't work that way. Emotions are powerful, and sometimes we feel overpowered by them. According to *Webster's*, the root source of the word *emotion* is the Latin *ex-movere*, meaning "to move away." And that is exactly what emotions do. They move up from somewhere deep within us and then they move out and pressure us to follow them. An emotional person is one who tends to follow her feelings most of the time. Emotional people think, speak, and act according to feelings. God has a good plan for our lives, but we do have an enemy named Satan, and his desire is that we follow all our feelings and end up in ruin.

The dictionary also says that an emotion is "a complex, usually strong subjective response...involving physiological changes as a preparation for action." Emotions drive us to take some kind of action. When we experience intense emotion, it is difficult not to follow our emotions, but if what they are leading us to do is wrong, then we must say no to them.

Think of a situation that makes you impatient and remember how you feel when that occurs. If you're like me, you want to lash out at somebody or something. But experience teaches us that we will later on regret most of what we say when we are feeling impatient. The key is to learn to live with impatient feelings and wait for the emotions to subside before deciding on any course of action.

I recently canceled an appointment twenty-four hours in advance, per the business's cancellation policy. On the day of the appointment, about five minutes after the planned appointment time, I received a call asking if Joyce Meyer was going to keep her appointment. I stated that we had canceled it, but the girl on the other end of the phone assured me they did not make mistakes like that and the appointment had not been canceled. She further told me that the bill for their services would be charged to my credit card. I definitely had emotion rise up and start to move out. I tried to use my nicest impatient voice and told her that we had canceled for sure and she was not to charge my account with anything. She told me once again that we had not canceled and unless we could prove that we had, she would have to bill me.

Since I was ready to explode, I told her that I would have the person call who had canceled the appointment for me. I also told her that I had given them a lot of business in the past, and it was rather foolish to tell me I was not telling the truth about the cancellation. My assistant assured me that the appointment had been canceled, and after two more calls and speaking to a manager, the situation was straightened out. The office apologized for the mix-up and said they would not be charging my account and looked forward to my business in the future.

Had I said everything to the girl on the phone that I felt like saying, I would have made a fool of myself. I felt like yelling at her, but I was able to be quiet, take a breath, pray, and make a decision that even if I ended up getting charged for the appointment, I was not going to lose my peace over it. I knew if they cheated me, God would take it away from them and get it back to me, even if He went through thousands of people to do it. I would like to say that I have handled situations that well all my life, but I haven't. Many times I have wished I would not have said or done a certain thing, but I have learned that I can have a feeling that is very strong and still not let it force me to say or do things that would be improper.

When the emotions of a situation are more than you can control properly, it is best to get away from it, even if it's only for a few minutes. That will give you time to think and have a chat with yourself. Thoughts do affect emotions, so having a talk with yourself is helpful. Remember all the other times you have behaved and spoken from emotion and all the trouble and embarrassment it caused. Then ask yourself if you really want to go around that same mountain again.

Nobody will ever reach a place in life where they don't experience a wide variety of negative emotions. If we get hurt, we feel angry. We don't feel like being around the person who hurt us. We feel like shutting them out of our lives. We feel guilty about mistakes we make; we feel impatient if

we are not getting our way; we feel frustrated if we are trying to accomplish something and all our efforts are thwarted.
We may feel enthusiastic and passionate or cold and uninter-
ested. Some of the emotions that we experience are pleasant
and to be desired, yet others are very unpleasant.

Feelings Do Not Need Our Permission to Show Up or Go Away

Our emotions tend to ebb and flow like ocean waves. It
would be so nice if they would just ask permission to come
or go, but they don't. They just do their own thing, and without any warning. Wishing our emotions were different won't
change a thing, so we need to do more than wish. We need to
learn all we can about them and take proper action to manage them. If we take the trouble to observe ourselves, we will
easily perceive how quick to change our feelings are.

A rebellious child does a lot of things without a parent's
permission, and just wishing that the child wouldn't do that
won't change a thing. The parent must discipline the child to
bring about change. The same principle holds true with emotions. They are often like rebellious children, and the longer
they are allowed to do as they please, the more difficult it
will be to control them.

My daughter, Sandy, and her husband, Steve, have eight-
year-old twin girls. Steve and Sandy have studied parenting
techniques and one thing they work with their children on
a lot is self-control. It's interesting to watch how it works
for them. One or both of the girls may be behaving quite

emotionally. They might be angry or acting selfish, and one of the parents will say, "Girls, let's get some self-control. Come on, let me see self-control." That's the girls' signal to fold their hands in their laps and sit quietly until they calm down and can behave correctly. It works beautifully! It will be easier for the twins, Angel and Starr, to manage their emotions as adults because they are learning to do so early in life.

I spent the first fifteen years of my life in a house where emotions were volatile, and it seemed normal to me to let them rule. I learned that if you didn't get what you wanted, you yelled, argued, and stayed angry until you got your way. I learned how to manipulate people by making them feel guilty. I learned starting at an early age to be emotional, and it took lots of years to unlearn what I had learned. I encourage you to control yourself and teach your children at an early age how to do the same thing. If it is too late for that, then begin where you are now, because it is never too late to do the right thing.

I think one of the reasons why so many people are emotionally controlled is simply because nobody has ever fully explained to them that their feelings are merely one part of their beings and should not be allowed to be their boss. We have to learn how to be led by the Spirit and not the soul. I cringe when I remember all the years I lived without knowing I didn't have to follow my feelings. I did so many unwise things during those years. They were wasted years that I cannot get back, but I can help others by teaching them what I have learned.

The Bible says in Psalm 1:1 that we are not to take counsel from the ungodly. I believe that taking advice from our feelings fits into that category and is a big mistake. Feelings are simply fickle; they change frequently and you just can't trust them. We can hear a good speaker talk about the volunteers needed at church and be so moved that we sign up to help, but that doesn't mean we will feel like showing up when it is our turn to work. If we sign up and then don't show up because we just don't feel like it, we become people without integrity and our actions don't honor God. This is a huge problem in our society today, and I believe it weighs much heavier on the inner person than we realize. When we don't keep our word, we know it isn't right. And no matter how many excuses we make, it sits in our consciences like a weight. We may make an excuse for it, but it's like sweeping dirt under the carpet. It's still there, and if we do it often enough, the dirt becomes impossible to hide.

If we desire to walk after the Spirit, all our actions must be governed by principles. In the realm of the Spirit there is a precise standard of right and wrong, and how we feel does not alter that standard. If doing the right thing requires a yes from us, then it must be yes whether we feel excited or discouraged. If it is no, then it is no. A principled life is enormously different from an emotional life. When an emotional person feels thrilled or happy, he may undertake what he ordinarily knows is unreasonable and unwise. But when he feels cold and emotionless or melancholy, he will not fulfill his duty because his feelings refuse to cooperate. All who desire to be truly spiritual must conduct themselves daily according to godly principles.

We should always count the cost to see if we have what it takes to finish a thing before we begin it. If we begin and find we cannot finish, then we definitely need to communicate openly and honestly with all parties involved. Even if you have to call someone and say, "I committed to that without really thinking about it properly, and now I find I cannot complete it," that is much better than just trying to ignore a commitment simply because you don't feel like fulfilling it. Our emotions will help us commit, but anyone who finishes always comes to a place where she has to press on without feelings to support her.

Don't Let Your Emotions Vote

Learn not to ask yourself how you feel about things, but instead ask yourself if doing or not doing something is right for you. You may know that you need to do something, but you don't feel like doing it at all. You can wish you felt like it, but as we discussed already, wishing does no good. You must live by principle and simply choose to do what you know is right. There may be a certain thing you want to do badly. It might be a purchase you want to make that you know is too expensive. Your feelings vote yes, but your heart says no. Tell your feelings they don't get to vote. They are too immature to vote and will never vote for what is best for you in the long run.

We don't allow people to vote in political elections until they are eighteen because we assume they would be too immature to know what they were doing. Why not look at your emotions the same way? They have always been a part of you, but they are very immature. They are without wisdom and cannot be trusted to do the right thing, so just don't let them vote. We mature but our emotions don't, and if they are left unchecked, our lives will be a series of unfinished and disappointing ventures.

People frequently ask me how I feel about traveling so much in my ministry. I have simply learned to say, "I don't ask myself." If I asked myself too often, I would find that I don't like it much and might be tempted to stop doing something I believe God wants me to do. Someone asked me a few months ago if I was excited about an upcoming trip to Africa and I said, "I have something better than excitement: I am committed." I didn't feel excited about going because I've been there several times and I know how I will feel when I return home after being in an airplane for many hours. But I do know that I am called by God to help the people, and in order to do that I have to travel. So I am led not by excitement or the lack of it—I just go! I am fulfilled and satisfied in knowing that I have obeyed God and helped other people.

When traveling was new to me, it was very exciting, but most things we do frequently are no longer exciting to us. However, the loss of the emotion of excitement does not mean we are not supposed to do those things anymore.

Where's the Thrill?

I wonder how many millions of people think, *I just don't feel the way I once did about my husband or wife. I wish I still felt excited about our marriage—that the romantic feelings would come back.* Just a reminder: wishing does no good; only action changes things. If you don't feel you are getting anything out of your marriage, perhaps you are not putting enough into it. I say that only because that was what God told me once when I was complaining about what I felt I wasn't getting from Dave. What God said was not what I wanted to hear, but it was true. He said, *Joyce, if you want more out of your marriage, put more into it.* I may not have liked hearing that, but I knew He was right.

We usually give our spouses the responsibility of making us happy rather than living to make them happy. In the process, neither one ends up happy. But you can change that! If you want your marriage or any other relationship to improve, just start doing more of the right thing yourself.

Don't have unrealistic expectations. Recognize the feelings you had in the early days of your relationship for what they were. They were feelings—no more, no less—just feelings! When I married Dave, I didn't even know what love was, and my emotions were so dysfunctional that whatever I did feel couldn't have been trusted to tell me anything. I married Dave because he asked me to, and I knew he was a good man. He did excite me because he was and is very good-looking. He was also an amateur bodybuilder and had muscles everywhere. I liked the way I felt when he kissed me. He had a car and I didn't have one. He had money and I didn't have any, so there were lots of things to excite me. We have been married forty-four years now, and I can say without any hesitation that I sincerely and definitely love Dave. I don't always feel excited when he comes home, my heart doesn't pound when he kisses me, but I truly do love him.

No matter what happens, I am committed to Dave. That

is love! Love is not a mere feeling. It is a decision about how we will behave and treat people.

Love can produce feelings, and I am not saying that feelings aren't enjoyable, because if they are good ones, they're very enjoyable! But I *am* saying that feelings cannot be depended upon and they don't always tell the truth.

A woman told me recently that she loved another man and did not love her husband anymore. I am trying to get her to understand that even if she chooses the other man, her feelings toward him will eventually change too. Then she'll be left with no good feelings, and lots of negative feelings of guilt, shame, and failure. If the man she has feelings for is willing to cheat on his wife, then he is likely to cheat on her also. His character is not too admirable, if you ask me. On the other hand, her husband is willing to forgive her and wants the marriage to work. That alone shows me that he does have character because he is willing to set aside his own wounded feelings and disappointment in order to save his marriage.

The woman in question *feels* she can never be happy without the other man, but I know for a fact, from the Word of God and life's experiences, she will never be happy with him either. Once the excitement of having the forbidden fruit wears off, the misery will begin.

Just look at Adam and Eve in the garden. Satan made the fruit look like something Eve just could not pass up. She had to have it, and I am sure it excited her to think about what she thought it would bring her. Satan said that if she ate it, she would be like God! But the moment she ate and gave the fruit to Adam and he ate, they both lost something they never got back. They were ashamed and felt guilty and they hid from God. Doing the wrong thing, no matter how excited it makes us feel, absolutely cannot produce lasting joy. I urge all my readers to choose now what you will be happy with later on. Make decisions based not on excitement or the lack of it, but on God's principles.

The nature of the flesh is to want what it thinks it cannot have, but once it has what it thought it wanted, the craving starts all over again. The one word that the flesh screams the loudest is *more*, and no matter how much it has, it is still never satisfied.

Most of us make a lot of mistakes before we find this out, so I hope you have already experienced enough in life to be able to say, "Amen, Joyce. I know that is right." But if you haven't had enough experience of your own, then please listen to me and avoid a lot of pain in life.

Decision and confession: *When I need to make a decision, I won't let my emotions vote.*

CHAPTER
6

Do You Have a Pulse?

We have been talking mainly about people who have lots of feelings and live by them, but have you ever met someone and thought, *Do you even have a pulse?* There are people who don't seem to feel much of anything. In some ways life is easier for them, but cold emotion must be controlled the same as excessive emotion. The two main problems I see with people whose emotions are minimal are (1) they may not accomplish much in life unless they learn not to let their lack of strong feelings control them, and (2) they can be dull to live with. Just as the emotional person must learn to live by principle rather than emotion, the emotionless person must do the same. Whether we have too much or too little emotion, we cannot live according to it.

Some people may be emotionally cold because they've been hurt in life and have become hardened and desensitized. They don't want to feel because they learned early on that feeling is often painful. They have developed ways to deny or turn off their feelings. Many of these people have addictive behaviors. I recently watched a television show about a woman who was a hoarder. She absolutely could not get rid of anything. Her stuff made her feel secure. This addiction was destroying her family and her life, so she sought professional counseling. The goal of all counseling is to get to the root problem that is causing the excessive behavior, and they discovered what hers was. During her childhood years, her father had a job that required her family to move almost yearly. Each time they moved, she lost her friends and had to leave behind most of her possessions that she had become attached to. She remembered one particularly painful experience, watching her father burn some of the toys and possessions she was very fond of. Her father should have been more sensitive to her reaction to how he handled the moves, but he wasn't. He could have allowed her to keep a few of the things that were the most important to her, but sadly, a lot of adults think only of themselves when making decisions that affect the entire family, and they leave a trail of wrecked and wounded people behind them.

As an adult, she associated getting rid of anything with pain and unpleasant memories, so she simply held on to everything. Her entire home looked like one giant trash can. She was addicted to stuff and used that addiction to control feelings of pain connected to loss. As she began to clean out her house with her family members and counselors and get rid of a lot of her possessions, she felt a lot of emotional pain. But she also enjoyed the feeling of freedom she was experiencing. She understood that her healing would not come overnight or easily, but she was determined to overcome her addiction. I am happy for that woman because I love to see people confront their problems, tear down walls of bondage, and learn to enjoy freedom. I suggest that you stop right now and ask yourself if you have any self-made walls that need to come down in your own life.

Many people who seem to be cold and emotionless have merely developed ways to numb their pain. They may have become masters at isolation. They feel safe only when they are not involved with anyone. After all, they cannot get into trouble or face rejection if they do nothing and say nothing. In my case, I had been hurt so much in my childhood that I became a control freak in order to keep people from hurting me. I thought if I stayed in control I would be safe. A wonderful Bible teacher and author named Lisa Bevere wrote a book called *Out of Control and Loving It*. I like that title, and I immediately knew when I saw it what Lisa was trying to convey. When we feel we must control everything and everyone, we are usually stressed to the max all the time. After all, running the entire world is hard work. But if we learn to control ourselves rather than trying to control other people, we will more easily love and enjoy life.

People who don't exhibit much emotion need healing just as excessively emotional people do. Anytime we discover that we are out of balance in an area of life, we need to confront it and work with the Holy Spirit to bring it into balance. If one is too emotional, she needs to be less so; and if one is emotionless, he needs to stir himself up a bit. If a person talks too much, she needs to learn how to be quiet. But if someone is too quiet, he needs to learn to make conversation for the sake of relationship and a well-balanced social life.

People who have been hurt often build walls that they hide behind to protect them-selves. But I have learned in life that if I wall oth-ers out, I also wall myself in, and I lose my free-dom.

> *I have learned in life that if I wall others out, I also wall myself in, and I lose my freedom.*

dom. I am a strong believer in tearing down unhealthy walls and letting God become our wall of protection.

> Violence shall no more be heard in your land, nor devasta-tion or destruction within your borders, but you shall call your walls Salvation and your gates Praise.   *(Isaiah 60:18)*

This beautiful scripture brings us a wonderful promise. Salvation through Jesus becomes our wall of protection. We no longer need to live lives full of violence, devastation, and destruction.

Another scripture tells us that if we don't have self–control, we are like a broken-down city without walls (see Prov. 25:28). So no matter how many walls we think we are building to protect ourselves, if we do not maintain balanced emotions, all our walls are mere illusions and not walls that protect us at all.

> *The walls we build around us to keep sadness out also keep out the joy.*
> Jim Rohn

> The walls we build around us to keep
> sadness out also keep out the joy.
> *Jim Rohn*

That's Just the Way I Am

Some people are quiet, shy, and more laid-back simply because of their personality. I am a talker and my husband is not, and there is nothing wrong with either of us. But when anything becomes excessive to the point that it is hindering our freedom or hurting other people, we cannot say, "That's just the way I am." Dave needs to talk to me more than he might prefer to at times because that's what I need, and love requires that we make sacrifices for the sake of other people. There are also times when I would like to rattle on and on in conversation, but I notice that Dave isn't really enjoying it so I decide to be quiet or I go find someone else to talk to.

We must work with God to find the balance between being who we are and not excusing rude or unloving behavior by saying, "That is just the way I am." God is in the business of changing us into His image, and that means He helps us control our weaknesses and He uses our strengths.

Dave and I have very different personalities, and yet we get along fabulously. It was not always that way, but we've learned to be what the other needs and yet not go so far that we lose our own freedom. I try to meet Dave's needs and he does the same thing for me. Dave likes things that I don't enjoy, but I still encourage him to do them so he can feel fulfilled, and he treats me the same way. When a friend or spouse needs you to adapt in some area to make the relationship better, it is foolish and selfish to say, "Sorry, that is just the way I am." We may be more comfortable and find it easier to do what we feel like doing, but we can make adjustments and still not lose our individuality.

The apostle Paul said that he learned to be all things to all people in an effort to win them to Christ (see 1 Cor. 9:19–22). In other words, he adapted to his surroundings rather than expecting everything and everyone to adapt to him. I am sure his decision allowed him to enjoy a lot of peace and gave him many more friends. We can make ourselves very miserable and have stress-filled lives by never being willing to change or adapt. We are all different, but we can get along peacefully.

As I mentioned earlier, my husband's personality is mainly phlegmatic, and mine is choleric. Those personalities are opposites, but we complement each other when we walk in love. I make decisions very quickly and Dave tends to want to think about things a long time. I flow more out of instinct, but he uses more logic and reason. The truth is that we need both in order to make consistently good decisions, so God gives each of us a part of what is needed and wants us to lean on each other and work together. I have gotten better at waiting over the years but will never be as naturally good at it as Dave is. Choleric people do everything quickly, and phlegmatic people do things more slowly and deliberately. I can clean up the kitchen quicker than Dave can, but he will do it better because he's more precise in what he does.

We have twenty people in our immediate family. That includes Dave and me, our four children and their spouses, and ten grandchildren. We are close and spend a lot of time together, yet we have a wide variety of personalities among the twenty of us. My two sons and I are full-on choleric, and all three of us are married to wonderful phlegmatic people. One of our daughters is phlegmatic, as well as two sons-in-law and one grandson. Of course other family members possess even different blends of personality. One daughter is melancholy, sanguine, and choleric. My point is that we have quite a variety of people who all view things differently and need different things to sense fulfillment.

My daughter who is melancholy requires compliments from her phlegmatic husband, who frequently forgets to give them. He thinks she is beautiful but might not even think to make the effort to say so. They have discussed this several times, and he finally started making reminder notes on his calendar. The more laid-back, emotionless person needs to find ways to remind himself to do what needs to be done. There have been plenty of times in my life when I have had to actually make notes in my journal reminding myself to not talk too much or to mind my own business or to not come across as controlling. If the loud, more aggressive people have to tone it down a bit, I think it is only fair for the quiet, less emotional, and nonaggressive people to find ways to stir themselves up. I can look at a very nonaggressive person and think, *Do you even have a pulse?* and of course they do; it just beats a little slower than mine does.

Many marriages fail because people won't make an effort to give their spouse what he or she needs. We tend to think that if we don't need something, then nobody does. Or if a person does have a need that is different from our own, we tend to belittle that need. That kind of attitude is one of the quickest ways to ruin a relationship. Thank God that in our family we've learned and are still learning that everyone's needs are valid—even if a need is hard to understand or difficult for us to meet.

Love demands that we all be willing to grow and change. That process is a bit more difficult for people who are more laid-back and easygoing. Changing takes work, and sometimes they just don't want to make the effort or even see the need. To be honest, I reached a point in life where I became weary of thinking I needed to be less aggressive, while all the people who appeared to me to have no pulse were applauded for never making any waves. If your personality is phlegmatic, you might want to make more of an effort to participate in what is going on around you and be enthusiastic about it. If you are really, really quiet, you might want to make an effort to speak up a bit more, even if it is not the most comfortable thing for you. Your talking more is not any harder than my talking less! Try to get excited along with the people you care about who are enthusiastic about their latest plan or project. It is one of the ways you can show love.

I remember coming home with excitement about my latest goal or plan and feeling like Dave threw ice water on all my enthusiasm. His response was more logical, but it was not good for our relationship. He may have needed to balance me out a bit, but I needed him to join me in my dream. He has learned to do so, and I have learned not to have a new dream or goal four times a day. One day he said, "You are the visionary and I am the pro-visionary," so we look at things from two different angles. I sometimes think about just my enthusiasm for completing the goal, but Dave has to think about how we are going to achieve it. God said that when a man and a woman are married, the two will become one flesh, but

He never said it would be easy. Good relationships require a lot of hard work, education, and willingness to meet each other's needs.

I Just Don't Care

The truth is that more-aggressive people care about a lot of things that less-aggressive people don't care about at all. We eat out often, and frequently out of respect I will ask one of my easygoing family members where they would like to eat or what they would like to eat. And they usually say, "It doesn't matter; I don't care what I eat." This amazes me because I always care where and what I eat and cannot fathom a person not caring what they eat. I know to the exact teaspoonful how much cream I want in my coffee and what temperature it should be. I would never say, "Just give me coffee with some cream, please." I would say, "Coffee with cream on the side so I can put it in myself."

I love going to Starbucks because they have great customer service. They will customize your coffee order so it is precisely what you want, and if they make it wrong, they are usually happy to do it again. My order has morphed over the years and goes something like this: "A large coffee, and could you make a fresh pot? I would like it in this double-wall insulated cup that I brought in with me, and I need hot water on the side and half-and-half in another cup. I would like the coffee extra hot." While I am waiting for my order I hear many people say, "Coffee, please." I can't imagine making it that simple. A lot of people order in the drive-through, but that is something I would never do because I want to watch my order being made so I know I am getting exactly what I want. I cannot imagine not caring!

I love the stability and adaptability of the less-aggressive members of our family, and I desperately need them. If all twenty of us were like my two sons and me, we might kill one another. The bottom line of what I am trying to say is that we all need one another and should appreciate the relationships God gives us.

I know people who can wear the same outfit twice a week every week for ten years and not care, but I won't wear the same pajamas two nights in a row. I need a lot of variety, but our beloved phlegmatic people just don't care. My phlegmatic daughter sleeps in an old undershirt, but I want to look cute when I go to bed. She doesn't care what she looks like in bed, but I care what I look like everywhere!

If we can learn which battles to fight and which ones to leave alone, we might win the war. For example, although God has changed me a lot, I will probably always be a little bossy. Dave knows that, so he doesn't fight the battle of trying to change me. He knows my heart and lets me be who I am. In restaurants I sometimes (actually quite often) suggest what he might want to eat. I am so good at making decisions that I thoroughly enjoy making them for everyone. He listens to me, and if my suggestion suits him he orders it, and if it doesn't he just gets what he wants. He could get upset and tell me to stop trying to tell him what to do and then I could get my feelings hurt, and we could waste an entire day being angry at each other, but we have learned that type of behavior is useless. We've gotten to the point where our differences amuse us rather than upset us.

Instead of resenting the fact that people are not like us and trying to change them, we should strive to get along and trust God to change what needs to be changed in each of us.

Even when you think someone has no pulse, I can assure you they do. It just beats a bit slower than other people's. Loving people unconditionally is the greatest gift we can give them and ourselves. I have learned that one of the secrets to my own personal peace is letting people be who God made them to be, rather than trying to make them be who I would like them to be. I do my best to enjoy their strengths and be merciful toward their weaknesses because I have plenty of my own. I don't need to try to take the speck out of their eye while I have a telephone pole in my own.

A woman I know was widowed not long ago, and she was telling me about her relationship with her husband. This woman is pretty strong-willed and likes things to go her way. She told me that when she was first married, she noticed a lot of things about her husband that annoyed her. Like any good wife, she told her husband about his annoying traits and habits so he could change.

Gradually it dawned on her that although she was very good about telling her husband all the things about him that needed to change, he never returned the favor! As she wondered why, she realized that somewhere along the line, her husband had made a decision not to look at—or for—her flaws. He knew she had plenty! But he wasn't going to focus on them. It occurred to her that she could continue to point out all his annoying traits—or she could choose not to. Just as her husband had done.

At the end of our conversation, she told me that in the twelve years they were married, her husband never said an unkind word to her. I think we can all take a lesson from that.

Cast Your Care

Casting the whole of your care [all your anxieties, all your worries, all your concerns, once and for all] on Him, for He cares for you affectionately and cares about you watchfully.   *(1 Peter 5:7)*

Obeying this scripture is a bit more difficult for those of us who care about most everything and a lot easier for those blessed and less-emotional people. Because I care about most things in life and want them to go a certain way, my care can easily turn into worry if I am not careful. God has worked in and with me for years, and I can honestly say that I rarely ever worry now, but it took me a long time to learn not to try to do something about things I could not do anything about.

For example, I really can't do anything about what people think of me, so being overly concerned about it is a total waste of time and energy. My husband certainly does not care what people think of him. On occasion when I have asked him how he feels about some negative thing someone has said about us, he tells me he doesn't feel anything, but instead he just trusts God to take care of it. I have gotten very upset at times when unkind articles have been written about me in the newspapers or we have been judged unfairly, but Dave just says, "Cast your care."

We have had a lot of arguments in the past over that statement. I want him to share my feelings, but he really can't because he simply isn't bothered by the things that bother me. I know he is right when he tells me to cast my care, but since I am already in the midst of caring, that is not the answer I want. Thankfully, God has helped me and continues to do so, and Dave has been a good example to me. But I have to work at not caring more than he does.

If you are a more emotional person, I'm sure the less emotional people in your life have frustrated you at times. Nothing seems to bother them and lots of things bother you. I get it! I have been there and I do know how you feel, but I have also lived long enough to realize that living by feelings is a big mistake. It is true that the best way to live is to learn to cast your care and let God care for you.

Decision and confession: *With God's help I can get along with and adapt well to all kinds of people.*

CHAPTER
7

Emotional Reactions

Do not [for a moment] be frightened or intimidated in anything by your opponents and adversaries, for such [constancy and fearlessness] will be a clear sign (proof and seal) to them of [their impending] destruction, but [a sure token and evidence] of your deliverance and salvation, and that from God. *(Philippians 1:28)*

Learning to act according to God's Word is much better than reacting emotionally to circumstances. It is admittedly not always easy, but it is possible; otherwise, God would not have instructed us to do so. In this chapter I want to examine four different areas. I encourage you to ask yourself honestly how you respond to them emotionally. The scripture above is one of Dave's favorites, and he quotes it often. If we can remain constant during the ever-changing tides of life and the unwanted circumstances life brings, we will please God and find that He always delivers us.

Change and Transition

Everything changes except God, and letting all the changes in our lives upset us won't keep them from occurring. People change, circumstances change, our bodies change, our desires and passions change. One certainty in life is change. We don't mind change if we invite it, but when it comes uninvited, our emotions can easily flare up.

John worked for an investment company for thirty-two years and was sure he would retire from that company. Without warning, the company decided to sell to a larger firm, whose management decided they didn't want to keep a lot of the employees, and John lost his job. He feels that he wasn't treated fairly when he was let go. Now what? John has a choice to make. He can either react emotionally by getting upset, stressed out, anxious, angry, and worried, feeling and saying lots of negative things. Or he can act on God's Word and trust God to be his vindicator and source of supply for every need. It is totally understandable that John has these emotions, but if he chooses to react based on his feelings, then he will be miserable and possibly make the other people in his life miserable. If he chooses to make decisions based on God's Word, however, he can make the transition with far less turmoil. Would his anger dissipate right away? Probably not. But if John truly gives his care over to God, his feelings will calm down and he can be confident that God will continue to work in his life, bringing justice for the injustice done to him.

Most changes take place without our permission. But we

can choose to adapt. If we refuse to make the transition in our minds and attitudes, then we are making a huge mistake. Our refusal to adapt doesn't change the circumstances, but it does steal our peace and joy. Remember, if you can't do anything about it, then cast your care and let God take care of you.

For quite some time, Dave has met some of his friends a couple of times a year to play golf for three days. It has been something he really enjoys, but over the past couple of years he has found it necessary to make some changes. There was a time when he and his friends played fifty-four holes of golf for two days and then thirty-six holes the last day, but those days are past. It has become harder physically for him to do that. He's in great physical shape, but nonetheless, he is seventy years old and very simply doesn't have the same level of endurance he once had.

While I was writing this book, Dave and his friends went to Florida for one of their trips. When Dave returned home he said to me, "This was the last time I'm doing this." He told me how much hassle and effort it was to get there, and that by the second day his back was tight and he had to ride in the cart and not play part of the time. In addition to that, he was wearing a knee brace because one of his knees was bothering him. He said he would have rather been home. His body is changing, so he mentally transitioned. He told me, "I will still be able to play, but now I will just do it a different way. The guys can come to St. Louis so I don't have to travel because they are younger than me. We can play thirty-six holes instead of fifty-four the first two days and eighteen holes the last day." That still sounds pretty intense to me, but for him it was a big change. His body is changing, and he is changing with it and keeping a good attitude about it.

Dave could have had a "male ego episode" and refused to admit that he was not able to do the golf trips anymore in the same way he has always done them. He could have gotten upset and decided he didn't like getting older and all that goes with it. But instead he acted on God's Word and made the transition gracefully. He realizes the day will come when he may need to make more changes, and he has already set his mind that when it does come, he will do so with a good attitude.

Since Dave enjoys his golf tremendously, I asked him how he would handle it if for some reason he could not play anymore, and his answer was amazing. He said, "I would probably be disappointed, but I would remember all the years I did get to play and be thankful for that. I would adapt and find something else to do."

Learn to Adapt

Readily adjust yourself to [people, things] and give yourselves to humble tasks. Never overestimate yourself or be wise in your own conceits.   (Romans 12:16)

In the previous chapter we discussed adapting to the different personalities we encounter in life. Now we are discussing adapting to changing circumstances that we cannot do anything about. How we respond emotionally determines how much peace and joy we have. Our thoughts are the first thing we need to deal with during change, because thoughts directly affect emotion. When circumstances change, make the transition mentally, and your emotions will be a lot easier to manage. If something changes that you are not ready for and did not choose, you will more than likely have a variety of emotions about it, but by acting on God's Word and not merely reacting to the situation, you will be able to manage your emotions instead of allowing them to manage you.

If you have read my other books or watched me on television, you already know that I strongly recommend confessing the Word of God out loud. Even though what you confess may be the opposite of how you feel, keep doing it. God's Word has inherent power to change your feelings. God's Word also brings comfort to us and quiets our distraught emotions. If you haven't read my previous book *Power Thoughts*, I recommend that you do. It gives an in-depth understanding of the power of our thoughts and words over circumstances and emotions.

How do you respond to change? Do you act on God's Word or merely react to the situation? After the initial shock, are you willing to make a transition mentally and emotionally?

Disappointed? Get Reappointed

Disappointment occurs when our plans are thwarted by something we had no control over. We can be disappointed by unpleasant circumstances or by people who let us down. We may feel disappointment with God when we've been expecting Him to do something and He doesn't. There are even times when we are disappointed in ourselves. Absolutely nobody gets everything they want all the time, so we need to learn how to deal properly with disappointment.

When we are disappointed, our emotions initially sink, and then sometimes they flare up in anger. After some time goes by and we have thoroughly expressed our anger, we may feel the sinking of emotions again. We feel down, negative, discouraged, and depressed. The next time you are disappointed, pay attention to the activity of your emotions, but instead of letting them take the lead, make the decision to manage them. There is nothing unusual or wrong about initial feelings of disappointment, but it is what we do from that point forward that makes all the difference in the world.

I learned long ago that with God on our side, even though we will experience disappointments in life, we can always get "reappointed." If you or I have a doctor's appointment and he has an emergency and has to cancel, we simply make another appointment. Life can be that way too. Trusting that God has a good plan for us, and that our steps are ordered by Him, is the key to preventing disappointment from turning into despair.

A man's mind plans his way, but the Lord directs his steps and makes them sure.   (Proverbs 16:9)

Man's steps are ordered by the Lord. How then can a man understand his way?   (Proverbs 20:24)

These two scriptures have stabilized my emotions many times when I was in a hurry to get somewhere and found myself at a standstill in traffic on the highway. Initially, I get a sinking feeling, then I get aggravated, and then I say, "Well, since my steps are ordered by the Lord, I will calm down and thank God that I am right where He wants me." I also remind myself that God may be saving me from an accident farther down the road by keeping me where I am. Trusting God is absolutely wonderful because it soothes our wild thoughts and emotions when things don't go the way we had planned.

How do you react when you get disappointed? How long does it take for you to make a transition and get reappointed? Are you acting on the Word of God or merely reacting emotionally to the circumstance? Are you controlled by what is around you, or by Jesus, who lives inside you?

If we don't ask ourselves questions and answer them honestly, we will spend our entire lives never truly knowing ourselves. Remember, only the truth will make you free (see John 8:32).

Trusting God completely and believing that His plan for you is infinitely better than your own will prevent you from being disappointed with God. It is impossible to be miffed at someone you really believe has your best interest in mind. When you are angry you want to lash out at someone, but it is unwise to make God your target. He is the only One who can help you and truly comfort you; therefore, it is much better to run *to* Him in your pain than away from Him.

I Failed Myself

We expect certain things and behaviors from ourselves, and when we fail to live up to those standards, it's easy to get angry with ourselves. For some people, that anger is deep-seated and long-standing. It is good to have high expectations of yourself, but not unrealistic ones. Perfectionists especially have problems in this area. They want to be perfect—and they never will be. We can be perfect in heart, but we won't arrive at perfection in our performance as long as we are in flesh-and-blood bodies. Thankfully, we can grow spiritually and learn to behave better, but I want to encourage you to learn how to celebrate even your small victories instead of being angry with yourself. It is only natural to feel disappointed in ourselves when we fail, but once again we need to not let the disappointment turn into a deeper problem. Get reappointed by reminding yourself that God loves you unconditionally and is changing you little by little. Look at your progress instead of how far you have to go.

We all disappoint ourselves at times. A few years ago I behaved very badly in a relationship, and to this day I am still sorry about the way I acted. I was working with someone and our personalities did not blend well at all. After trying for several years to make it work, I finally realized that I needed to make a change for both our sakes. I kept putting it off because I didn't want to hurt the other person. The longer I waited, the more her weaknesses irritated me, and I am sure mine irritated her. Because I felt trapped, it made me angry, and I reacted to the way I felt instead of taking proper action and doing what I knew I really needed to do.

I thought my reason for the procrastination was noble: I just didn't want to hurt her. But no matter how noble my motive was, I was still disobeying the Holy Spirit's leading, and that always ends up bad. When the relationship ended, it was not pretty, and I know we both regretted it. I did all I knew to do to make things right, but it was one of those situations that simply could not be fixed and I felt really bad about it.

It took me awhile, but I finally received God's forgiveness and made every effort to learn from my mistake. Let me assure you that staying angry with yourself because you failed won't do any good. Are you disappointed with yourself? If you are, then right now is the time to let it go and get reappointed. It is time to stop living by how you feel.

Learning to Wait Well

> Let endurance and steadfastness and patience have full play and do a thorough work, so that you may be [people] perfectly and fully developed [with no defects], lacking in nothing.　(*James 1:4*)

If you have not developed patience, then having to wait may bring out the worst in you. At least that was the case with me until I finally realized my emotional reactions were not making things go faster. The *Vines Greek Dictionary* states that patience is a fruit of the Spirit that grows only when we are subjected to trials. We would all like to be patient, but we don't want to develop patience because that means behaving well while we are not getting what we want. And that's *hard*!

Some people are naturally more patient than others due to their temperament, but I have found that even very patient people have at least a few things that irritate them more than others. As you may have guessed, Dave is very patient. Waiting does not bother him all that much. He would be fine in the traffic jam on the highway, unless of course it was going to make him late for his golf tee time. He is a bit impatient with drivers on the road who do things he is sure he would never do. But since his personality is easygoing and adaptable, waiting isn't that hard for him. It was however, very hard for me for many years. I finally realized that God consistently allowed me to be put in situations where I had no choice but to wait, and He did it so I could develop patience.

Patience is extremely important for people who want to glorify God and enjoy their lives. If one is impatient, the situations they encounter in life will certainly cause them to react emotionally. The next time you have to wait on something or someone, instead of just reacting, try talking to yourself a little. You might think, *Getting upset will not make this go any faster, so I might as well enjoy the wait.* Then perhaps say out loud, "I am developing patience as I wait so I am thankful for this situation." By doing that, you will be acting on the Word of God rather than reacting to the unpleasant circumstance.

Each time we exercise patience, we strengthen it, just as we develop our muscles each time we exercise them. I get sore when I exercise, and it hurts, but I know it is helping me. We can look at exercising patience the same way. Don't merely think about how hard and frustrating it is, but think about how peaceful you will be when waiting never bothers you.

Do you wait well? How do you act when you're working with someone who is really slow at what they are trying to do? How does getting caught in a traffic jam affect you? What if someone takes the parking space you have been waiting for? The more intensely we want something, the more our emotions will act up if we do not get it. Sometimes what we want is simply more important to us than it should be, and we need to realize that and not behave childishly. Common sense tells us that it is rather foolish to get into a rage over a parking space or some of the other simple things people tend to get upset about. What situations are difficult for you? How do you behave emotionally when you have to wait? On a scale of 1 to 10, how well do you handle yourself when things don't go your way? I have found that honest answers to questions like these are helpful in making progress toward managing our emotions.

Getting Along with People Who Are Difficult to Get Along with

How do you react to people who are rude? Do you respond in love as the Word says we should, or do you join them in their ungodly behavior? Not one of us appreciates irritable and irritating people. One definition of rudeness is being abrupt and unpleasantly forceful. I think there are a lot of people in the world like that today, largely because of the stressful lives most people live. People are trying to do too much in too little time and have more responsibility than they can realistically handle.

When a clerk in a store is rude to me, I can instantly feel my emotions start to rise up. As I said earlier, emotions rise up and then move out, wanting us to follow them. When I feel that, I know I need to take action. I have to reason with myself and remember that the person being rude probably has a lot of problems and she may not even realize how she sounds. I certainly remember lots of times in my life when people asked me why I was being so harsh and I didn't even realize that I was. I just had a lot going on and felt pressured, so the pressure escaped in harsh voice tones. That did not excuse my bad behavior, but it was the root of the problem.

I am very thankful that I know the Word of God and have Him in my life to help and comfort me. But I try to remember that a lot of people in the world who are difficult to get along with don't have that. I always want my behavior to be a witness for Christ and not something that would make Him ashamed of me. That being the case, I have had to work very hard with the Holy Spirit in developing the ability to act on the Word of God when people are rude instead of merely reacting to them with behavior that matches or tops theirs.

Jesus said that we have done nothing special if we treat people well who treat us well, but if we are kind to someone who would qualify as an enemy then we are doing well (see Luke 6:32–35).

This area is actually a very big one and presents a situation that we will deal with on and off throughout all our lives. People are everywhere, and not all of them are pleasant. So we must make a decision about how we are going to react toward them. Will you act on the Word of God and love them for His sake? Or will you merely react emotionally and end up perhaps acting worse than they act? Have you ever let a rude person ruin your day? Make a decision that you will not ever do that again because when you do, you are wasting some of the precious time that God has given you. When a day is gone, you can never get it back, so I urge you not to waste it being emotionally distraught over someone you may never even see again.

If you are in a situation that requires you to be with one of these hard-to-get-along-with people every day, I urge you to pray for them instead of reacting emotionally to them. Our prayers open a door for God to work through. Sometimes when we pray, God will lead us to confront a person like that. I am not saying we just have to put up with the person's bad behavior, but remember that confrontation should still be done in the spirit of love.

Decision and confession: *I can patiently wait for the things I want in life, trusting God to bring them in His timing.*

CHAPTER
8

Thoughts Are Fuel for Feelings

You, Who try the hearts and emotions
and thinking powers, are a righteous God.
(Psalms 7:9)

The psalmist David speaks about emotions and thoughts in the same sentence because they are intimately linked to each other. We must understand the power of thoughts in order to learn how to manage our emotions.

One statistic says that although thousands of people make decisions at the first of the year to start exercising and they go pay money to sign up at a gym, only 16 percent of them actually show up and follow through. This is a perfect example of a situation where a person wanted to do something, made a decision to do it, and then allowed his thoughts and feelings to become a dictator in his life. God has given us free will, and the truth is that our thoughts and feelings cannot rule us if we don't let them, but most people don't know that.

One day in December, Mark looked at himself in the mirror after taking a shower and thought, *I've gained weight over the past couple of years and I'm out of shape. I really need to do something. But the holidays are coming, so I guess I'll just enjoy eating whatever I want until January. Then I'll start on a diet and exercise program.* Mark felt good about his decision and wanted to make a commitment so he went by the gym the next day and signed up. He gave a credit card number at the desk and agreed to pay $45 a month for the next year so he could use the facility. Mark left the gym feeling good about his decision.

He enjoyed eating all he wanted over the holidays and kept telling himself and other people that in January he was going on a diet-and-exercise program. January came, the holidays were over, and he woke up on the first Monday of the month and told himself, *I will go to the gym today.* He headed off to work and even took gym clothes and tennis shoes with him. At work that day he was invited to go to lunch and it happened to be his favorite restaurant. He thought, *This is going to be hard because they have that lasagna I love, and that sure doesn't fit into my diet plan.* It never occurred to Mark to just turn down the invitation if he felt he could not go there and stay on his diet. He just assumed that the temptation would be too much, and in reality, had already planned for failure.

The first mistake that Mark made was thinking that resisting the temptation to eat lasagna was going to be too hard for him to do. He could have thought, *I want to go to lunch with my friends, but I am going to stay on my diet. I can do it! I love their lasagna, but I can say no to it.* You see, our thoughts prepare us for action, and since Mark had already thought it would be hard for him, when he got into the restaurant and started staring at the lasagna on the menu, he could not resist the temptation because he had already decided mentally what he would do. His feelings hooked up with his thoughts, and the two of them together made his decision for him.

All the carbohydrates in the lasagna made Mark sleepy that afternoon and by the time he got off work he thought, *Maybe I'll wait and start exercising later this week. After all, I already messed up by eating the lasagna, and I am really tired today anyway.* Of course his feelings agreed with the plan to go home and rest. They assured him that they did not feel like exercising, and waiting until another day sounded wonderful.

April rolled around, and Mark still had not gone on a diet or started exercising. He tried a few times, but his thoughts and feelings always defeated him. The gym had charged his credit card each month as promised, and he had paid out $180 for something he wasn't using. When he thought about it, he felt guilty, but his mind offered some excuses: *I tried to exercise, but I just have too much going on in my life. I really would like to take better care of myself, but I don't have time. I have a lot of responsibility, but things will change eventually and I will get around to it.* He wished he had not signed that contract because now he was going to waste $540.

Each one of the thousands of people who sign up at a gym in January and never show up, go through some version of Mark's story. They let their thoughts and feelings control their decisions. They could have been successful in disciplining themselves if they had understood the power of thoughts and known they had the authority to choose their thoughts rather than just going with whatever happened to come to mind.

Talk Yourself into Success

Nobody is successful in any venture by just wishing they would be. Successful people make a plan and talk to themselves about that plan consistently. You can think things on purpose, and if you make what you

> *Nobody is successful in any venture by just wishing they would be. Successful people make a plan and talk to themselves about that plan consistently.*

think about what you want to do, your feelings may not like it, but they will go along. I slept great last night, and when I woke up at 5:00 a.m., I didn't feel like getting up. It was so cozy under the fluffy cover, and I felt like staying right there. But I had a plan regarding working on this book. I had decided how many hours I would write today and in order to do that I had to get up. I thought, *I am going to get up now*, and I exercised willpower and I got up!

Do you even pay any attention to what you are thinking? Do you make an effort to choose your thoughts or do you just meditate on whatever falls into your head, even if it is in total disagreement with what you have said you want out of life? You don't have to be trapped by negative thoughts. When your thoughts are going in a wrong direction, do you cast them down and out of your head as the Bible instructs (see 2 Cor. 10:5)? How much are you letting your thoughts and feelings rule you? If you don't like your answers to these questions, the good news is that you can change. As I have said for years, we are in a war and the mind is the battlefield. We either win or lose our battles based on winning the war in our minds. Learn to think according to the Word of God, and your emotions will start lining up with your thoughts.

If you have had years of experiencing wrong thinking and letting your emotions lead you, making the change may not be easy, and it will definitely require a commitment of study, time, and effort. But the results will be worth it. Don't say, "I am just an emotional person, and I can't help the way I feel." Take control. You can do it!

The Power of Believing the Best

The hurtful and disappointing things people do are among the things that tend to stir up our emotions. Since we cannot control what others do or a lot of the circumstances of our lives, we need to look for ways to quiet our emotions concerning those things. The Bible teaches us to always believe the best of every person (see 1 Cor. 13:7). If we let our thoughts lead us, they usually tend toward negativity. Sadly, the flesh without the influence of the Holy Spirit is dark and negative. We learn in God's Word that we have a mind of the flesh and a mind of the Spirit (see Rom. 8:5). If we let the mind of the flesh lead, we will be filled with death-like feelings and attitudes. But if we choose to let the mind of the Spirit lead, we will be filled with life and peace in our souls, and that includes peaceful and calm emotions. I urge you to choose what makes for peace because Jesus has called us to peace. He has left us His peace, but a life of emotional turmoil not only makes us miserable, it can also make us sick. Stress is the root cause of a large percentage of sickness and disease. Dis-ease causes disease!

I realized last year that most of my emotional turmoil comes about through people problems. I knew from experience that I could not control people and what they decided to do, so I began to pray about what I could do to not allow what they do to upset me. In answer to my prayers and through study of God's Word, I started obeying 1 Corinthians 13:7 by choosing to believe the best of everyone.

An employee recently said some very hurtful and potentially damaging things about some of my family members and the ministry. The first reaction was shock, then disappointment, then confusion because we could not understand her motive. Finally, anger came. I have made a commitment to peace and I refuse to let my emotions control me, so I acted on what the Word of God says, and I decided to believe the best. I thought, *She is hurting from a tragic situation in her own life and she probably is acting out of her own pain. I doubt that she even fully realized the potential impact of her words.* I started praying for her, and when people asked me what I thought, I told them I was surprised and didn't fully understand why she did it, but then I repeated my "thinking the best" idea. I noticed that each time I took that approach, it calmed me down emotionally and had the same effect on other people who were involved.

> *I've always believed that you can think positive just as well as you can think negative.*
> Sugar Ray Robinson

I've always believed that you can think positive
just as well as you can think negative.
Sugar Ray Robinson

I truly believe the Word of God is filled with powerful secrets. They are not things that are hidden, but are definitely things that have been ignored. I have read it for years: "Love always believes the best of every person" (see 1 Cor. 13:7). I have followed that advice in obedience to God, but only recently have I realized that thinking the best is equivalent to taking a spiritual nerve pill. Because our thoughts are connected to our emotions when we think good thoughts, we will feel good emotionally.

Even if a person's motive is terrible, I can still protect myself by believing the best. I am not responsible for another's actions and motives, but I am responsible for my reaction to that person's actions. I decided to believe that God was able to work good things out of what appeared to be a bad situation and that made me feel even better. Don't ever be convinced that you have to be out of control just because you cannot control the people and things around you. Learn to live the interior life instead of the exterior life, and you will enjoy pleasant thoughts and calm emotions.

> If your enemy is hungry, feed him; if he is thirsty, give him drink; for by so doing you will heap burning coals upon his head. Do not let yourself be overcome by evil, but overcome (master) evil with good.   (Romans 12:20–21)

The burning coals that the scripture mentions are not payback for what the enemy has done, they are actually the fire of love you are showing that eventually melts the hardness of your enemy's heart.

Eventually, the employee I mentioned above resigned, and we decided to go the extra mile and offer a good severance package so she would have time to heal from her own emotional tragedy before she needed to look for a job. We prayed with her and continue to pray for her and trust God to take what Satan wanted to use for harm and work it out for good (see Gen. 50:20).

This biblical secret of believing the best belongs to every child of God. All you need to do is follow God instead of feelings. When you do, the intensity of your feelings will weaken because you are not feeding them with negative thoughts. We have to make the decision while our feelings are still stirred up, but I promise you that they will calm down if you follow God's plan.

God has not left us defenseless in these situations. We are in the world, but He encourages us not to be of it. That means if we will obey Him, then we will be hidden in Him, a place where a thousand can come against us, but we won't need to fear.

A thousand may fall at your side, and ten thousand at your right hand, but it shall not come near you. Only a spectator shall you be [yourself inaccessible in the secret place of the Most High] as you witness the reward of the wicked.   *(Psalm 91:7–8)*

Out of Gas

If we need gasoline (fuel) for our automobile and pull into a station only to find a sign that reads SORRY, OUT OF GAS, we are disappointed, but we go look for another gas station. I think the devil needs to find an OUT OF GAS sign on our minds when he comes to cause trouble in our lives. He can always find someone who will entertain his poisonous thoughts, but you can let him know that it is not going to be you.

Think about things that make you happy. I could sit here right now and upset myself if I wanted to. All I'd need to do is take about fifteen or twenty minutes and think about my childhood. Then I could think of all the people in my life who have hurt and disappointed me. I could think of all the things that didn't work out the way I had hoped they would, then I could imagine that more bad things are probably on the way. If I did that, I can promise you I would start to feel emotionally down, then undoubtedly angry. Why would we choose to make ourselves miserable? Ask yourself why you would do that and then make a decision to never do it again.

The next time your emotions are sinking or flaring up, stop and ask yourself what you have been thinking or even talking about. If you do this, you will probably locate the root of your problem.

Do It or Be Miserable

Like most of us, you probably wish there was an easier way to live, but there isn't. So you might as well decide to do things God's way or be miserable. We usually try to take all the easy paths, but they all lead to destruction. The Bible describes those paths as "broad" because a lot of effort isn't required to remain on them. We are encouraged by God to take the narrow path, the more difficult one, but also the one that leads to life: "Strive to enter by the narrow door [force yourselves through it], for many, I tell you, will try to enter and will not be able" (Luke 13:24).

We have to make a strong effort to push through the negativity in the world, but if we will do our part, God will always do His. Not everyone is willing to make the effort. They are addicted to ease and simply flow with their feelings. I am writing this book with the hope that my readers won't be of the many who do not enter. Jesus died for us so we could have a wonderful, abundant life that is filled with peace, joy, power, success, and every good thing, but we must drink the cup that He drank. He was willing to go to the cross and pay for our sins even though physically, mentally, and emotionally it was very difficult. We too must be willing to do what is right, and our reward will surely come.

Study the Word of God regularly, and then when trouble comes, you will already have your spiritual tank full of fuel that will enable you to make right choices. Don't be the kind of person who prays or has time for God only when you feel like it or have a disaster. Seek God because you know you cannot navigate safely in this world without Him. Truly, we can do nothing of any value without Him.

You and I can let our minds drift aimlessly day after day and we can be controlled by our emotions, or we can choose to gird up our minds, choose our thoughts carefully, and manage our emotions. God has set before us life and death, good and evil, and has given us the responsibility of making the choice (see Deut. 30:19).

If you choose what is right when it still feels wrong, you will be growing spiritually and making progress toward the life you really want to enjoy. Doing what is easy means stagnation or, even worse, a regression of any progress that has been made in the past. God is never motionless. He is always moving, and He invites us to follow Him. I like to say, "Get in, get out, or get run over." Decide to be red hot on fire for God, or decide to be cold, but don't live in the deception of merely being lukewarm. We can move with God, but if we move against Him by ignoring His principles, we will reap what we sow and we will not like the harvest we get.

Science and the Brain

Dr. Caroline Leaf has been in the field of learning, intelligence, and brain research for more than twenty-five years. As a born-again Christian working in universities, she realized there was a link between science and the brain. She states that this became very real to her after reading my book titled *The Battlefield of the Mind*. She realized that I was discovering as a Bible teacher what she was also discovering as a scientist. She teaches from a scientific viewpoint how people can put new information into their brains by simply choosing new thoughts. Dr. Leaf has proven scientifically, by watching the activity of the brain during research, that we can replace damaging old thoughts with new ones. She states that the nerve cells in our brains resemble little trees with many branches.

During an interview on my television show, Dr. Leaf stated the following:

> I teach people to understand that a thought is a real thing. I think many people think that a thought is merely something out there that they can't feel or touch. But, it's actually a real thing. As you're thinking, you're actually building memories in your brain and the thoughts in your brain look like trees. The interesting thing is that if the thought is a good one, based on something positive, that it actually looks different in the brain than a negative thought does. The toxic thought, as I refer to them, will affect your entire body. They form a different type of chemical than a positive thought does. The toxic thought causes little thorns to grow on the branches in the nerve cells. These thorns are actually a little pocket of chemicals, and those chemicals are toxic. They squirt out their poison that can make you sick. The poison goes first to the heart and begins to choke it, then it goes to the immune system and breaks down your defenses and makes it easier for disease to germinate in your body.

I asked Dr. Leaf if we could do anything about the damage that has already been done, and she assured me that the answer is yes.

She said, "Within four days you can change your neural circuitry. Even as you're listening to me now, you're changing it. It takes four days to start taking the thorns off the trees. It takes twenty-one days to actually establish a memory without the thorns, and then you grow a new memory over the old one."

We learn from God's Word that we are to renew our minds and attitudes through study and meditating on God's Word, and through that renewal we can enter the good life God has planned for us. Dr. Leaf states that repentance and forgiving anyone we are angry at are the best ways to start getting the thorns off our branches. She also stated that even after all the thorns are gone, we can rebuild them by beginning to think negatively again. The renewing of the mind is a constant, lifelong process, and to be honest, we must work on it every day.

Decision and confession: *I always believe the best of every person, and I am very positive.*

CHAPTER
9

Words Are Fuel for Emotions

Words are fuel for emotions, just as thoughts are. As a matter of fact, our words give our thoughts verbal expression. It's bad enough to think something negative, but verbalizing negativity makes it even worse. The effect it has on us is inestimable. Oh, how I wish that everyone in the world understood the power of their words and would learn to discipline what comes out of their mouths. Words are containers for power, and as such they have a direct effect on our emotions.

> *Words are containers for power, and as such they have a direct effect on our emotions.*

Words fuel good moods or bad moods; in fact, they fuel our attitudes and have a huge impact on our lives and our relationships.

A man has joy in making an apt answer, and a word spoken at the right moment—how good it is! *(Proverbs 15:23)*

In Proverbs 21:23 we are told that if we guard our mouths and tongues, we will keep ourselves from trouble. Proverbs also tells us that "death and life are in the power of the tongue, and they who indulge in it shall eat the fruit of it [for death or life]" (18:21). The message cannot be any clearer than that. If we speak positive and good things, then we minister life to ourselves. We increase the emotion of joy. However, if we speak negative words, then we minister death and misery to ourselves; we increase our sadness, and our mood plummets.

Why not help yourself first thing every day? Don't get up each morning and wait to see how you feel and then rehearse every feeling to anyone who will listen. If you do that, you are giving your emotions authority over you. You become the servant of your emotions, and that is definitely not a good position to be in.

Sometimes Just Talking *Does* Make It So

Harry got up yesterday morning and felt a little down. He didn't understand why he felt the way he did, and he began to complain to his wife. He said, "I don't know why I feel so down today. I think I'm getting depressed. And this is not a good day for a bad mood because I have a presentation to make at work that will determine whether or not we get that new account I told you about." Throughout his shower and breakfast, he'd think, *I wish I felt happier, I'm feeling worse as the minutes tick by,* and *What a day to be in a lousy mood.* By the time Harry left for work, he was dreading the day.

On the way to the office, he hit a major traffic jam due to a broken traffic light. "Great! This is just great," he said to no one in particular. "This is all I need. Now, on top of how I feel, I'm going to be late. Just what I needed...more pressure." He got through the traffic and as he attempted to enter the parking garage he always used, he found the entrance blocked off with a sign advising that the parking space lines were being repainted that day. His frustration and sour mood sank even further. The more upset he became, the worse his mood got, and the worse his mood got, the more he said that fed it and made it even worse.

Harry finally got to his office and went over his notes one last time before making his way to the boardroom to meet the potential new client. Several minor things happened that aggravated him. One man said the room was cold and asked if the heat could be turned up. Harry was already hot!

He was just about to begin his presentation when someone got a call on his cell phone. Everything had to be put on hold while the entire group checked to make sure their phones were off. Harry was thinking things that were not nice, such as: *These stupid people, why didn't they think of that* before *the meeting began?* When he started his presentation, his tone of voice was a bit sharp. He didn't smile once during the presentation—it never occurred to him to.

By now Satan was influencing Harry's mind, mouth, mood, and attitude. The whole time he was giving his presentation he was thinking, *This is useless; they won't choose us. I'm doing a terrible job, and it is all because I just happened to wake up in a bad mood. I don't know why things like this happen. They always happen at the wrong time. I needed a good mood today and lots of joyful feelings, but instead I got depression. Why did I have to feel this way today of all days?*

Harry did not get the account, his boss was not pleased with him, and he was severely reprimanded for his attitude. He went back into his office, shut the door, and called his wife. Once again he rehearsed all his bad luck. He talked about it for forty-five minutes and then said he was so depressed he couldn't even talk anymore.

The story of Harry is fictional, but it's also classic; things like this happen to people all the time. But very few ever realize they could have turned the day around early in the morning by choosing to think on something good and say positive things no matter how they felt when they woke up. You and I can turn a bad mood around by talking about something happy. Talk about your blessings, or something you are looking forward to, and you will soon see your mood improve. I am not suggesting that you can control every emotion you have with your words, but I know from experience that you can help yourself. We can talk ourselves into a better mood when we need to.

Why do we feel the way we feel? Perhaps it is because we talk the way we talk!

The Wise Man's Mind
Instructs His Mouth

The Bible speaks of wise men and foolish men. It says that the fool's mouth is his ruin, and his lips are a snare (trap) to him (see Prov. 18:7). A person would need to be foolish indeed to use her own mouth and words to ruin her own life, but people do it all the time. Why? Simply because they don't understand the power of words. We know that our words impact other people, but do we realize that our words impact ourselves and our lives? Harry is a perfect example. His story may be fictional, but we all know people like Harry in real life who talk themselves into all kinds of bad situations.

It's no wonder Proverbs 17:20 tells us that "he who has a wayward and crooked mind finds no good, and he who has a willful and contrary tongue will fall into calamity."

One of the biggest mistakes we make is to think we have no control over how we feel or what we do. God has given us a spirit of discipline and self-control, and it is called *self-control* because God gives us this tool to control ourselves. We all have it, but do we use it? Anything we have but never use becomes dormant and powerless. Do you work out regularly? Why do you do that? You exercise to keep your bones and your muscles strong—to guard your health.

The writer of Proverbs also tells us that "he who guards his mouth and his tongue keeps himself from troubles" (21:23). *That* is a wise man.

Millions of people live miserable and unfruitful lives because they are deceived. They believe they are merely victims of whatever comes their way. If they wake up feeling depressed, they offer no resistance, but erroneously assume that they must behave the way they feel. I know this very well because I lived in this same type of deception for a large part of my life. If the deceived person is offended and feels angry, he usually expresses his anger and even hangs on to it as if it is a battle prize. It occurs to very few that they can let the anger go and trust God to take care of their vindication.

The world is filled with discouraged, downtrodden individuals who could make their situations better by simply choosing to continue on in hope. Once we learn the power of hope and practice it, it is a hard habit to break. Just as a person can form a habit of being discouraged each time things don't go her way, she can learn to encourage herself through hoping that a blessing is right around the corner.

What we say in difficult times determines how long the difficulty will last and how intense the difficulty will become. I am certainly not saying that we can control everything that happens to us by choosing right words to speak, but we can control how we respond to the things that happen to us, and choosing right thoughts and words helps us do that. You can't control the wind, but you can adjust the sails.

Say What You Say on Purpose

I have probably never written a book that did not include some teaching about the power of words, and I probably never will. That is how important this subject is, and I want you to take it seriously. There is a time to talk and a time to keep silent. Sometimes the best thing we can do is say nothing. When we do say something, it is wisdom to think first and be purposeful in what we say. If we truly believe that our words are filled with life or death, why wouldn't we choose what we say more carefully?

Even a fool when he holds his peace is considered wise; when he closes his lips he is esteemed a man of understanding.   *(Proverbs 17:28)*

I firmly believe that *if we do what we can do, God will do what we cannot do.* We can control what comes out of our mouths with the help of the Holy Spirit and by applying principles of discipline. Even when we talk about our problems or the things that are bothering us, we can talk about them in a positive and hopeful way.

I have been having some back problems, and my daughter Sandy called this morning to see how my back was. I told her it was still hurting, but that I was thankful it wasn't as bad as it could have been. I said, "I am sleeping well, and that is a positive thing." In other words, I didn't deny the problem, but I am making an effort to have a positive outlook. I am determined to look at what I do have and not just at what I don't have. I know in time the backache will be taken care of, and I believe that until then, God will give me the strength to do what I need to do.

In 1911, the *Mona Lisa* turned up missing and could not be found for two years. It had been stolen. But an interesting phenomenon of human nature occurred. In the two years of its absence, more people looked at the spot where it previously rested than had actually seen the painting in the two years prior to its theft.

Just like all those visitors to the Louvre, many of us spend our lives more concerned about what's missing than about what we have, and sadly we often talk more about our problems than we do our blessings. Talking about problems causes us to focus on them, and as I say often, "What we focus on becomes larger and larger." I believe that misery is an option! Things don't make us miserable without our permission.

Robert Schuller said, "The good news is that the bad news can be turned into good news when you change your attitude." And if you can't muster up a good attitude concerning something you're unhappy about, you can at least try to downplay the negative.

My friend Antoinette, who lives in New York, told me about something that occurred recently that upset her terribly. She was driving home from visiting relatives at the end of Memorial Day weekend. As she approached the George Washington Bridge, hundreds of cars bottlenecked as they approached a handful of toll booths. Traffic was moving very slowly, and as she was following a big SUV in front of her through a series of traffic cones, she heard a siren from behind, and a policeman told her through a megaphone to stop and get out of the car.

He proceeded to treat her like a criminal, barking orders for her to hand over her license, registration, and insurance papers and get back into her car. She had no idea what she'd done wrong, and politely asked him what the problem was. He ignored her question and started writing a ticket. A few minutes later he called her back to his car and said, "You saw those cones. Now you're going to court."

To make matters worse, the ticket had no fine, but it did have a court date—she was ordered to appear before a judge three weeks later. Now she would have to take time off from work to appear in court...and she didn't even know what she had done wrong!

She had been under a lot of pressure, and that incident set her off completely. She started crying, cried her way across the bridge, and was still crying when she arrived home half an hour later. Obviously, she was upset about more than just the ticket.

Normally, she would have told her friends and her colleagues at work about the incident, since it was the overriding memory of her holiday weekend. But over the next day or so, whenever she was tempted to tell the story, she stopped herself.

It occurred to her that talking about the incident would just reinforce her bad mood and upset her. So when her friends asked her about her weekend, she just talked about the good parts and didn't tell them about her encounter with the law.

Antoinette learned quite a lesson: by deciding not to talk about her troubles, she actually was able to keep her turmoil down to a minimum.

If you will make a decision that you are going to say as little as possible about your problems and disappointments in life, they won't dominate your thoughts and your mood. And if you talk as much as possible about your blessings and hopeful expectations, your frame of mind will match them. Be sure each day is filled with words that fuel joy, not anger, depression, bitterness, and fear. Talk yourself into a better mood! Find something positive to say in every situation.

A little boy was overheard talking to himself as he strutted through the backyard, wearing his baseball cap and toting a ball and bat: "I'm the greatest hitter in the world," he announced. Then he tossed the ball into the air, swung at it, and missed. "Strike one!" he yelled. Undaunted, he picked up the ball and said again, "I'm the greatest hitter in the world!" He tossed the ball into the air. When it came down he swung again and missed. "Strike two!" he cried. The boy then paused a moment to examine his bat and ball carefully. He spit on his hands and rubbed them together. He straightened his cap and said once more, "I'm the greatest hitter in the world!" Again he tossed the ball up into the air and swung at it. He missed. "Strike three! Wow!" he exclaimed. "I'm the greatest pitcher in the world!"

This boy had such a positive attitude that he concluded if he missed the ball three times, the only possible reason was that he was such a great pitcher even he could not hit his own pitching. He was determined to say something positive, and I strongly imagine that determination kept him from getting discouraged and in a bad, sad mood.

Decision and confession: *I will say positive, hopeful things no matter how I feel.*

CHAPTER
10

Can I Control Something for a Change?

It's no wonder that we humans want to control things… there's so much that's *out* of our control. But unfortunately, rather than bothering to try to control ourselves, we usually try to control what we should not try to control. I spent years trying to control the people in my life as well as all my circumstances because I was afraid of being hurt or taken advantage of. But the only thing I achieved was constantly being frustrated and angry. It took me a long time to realize that people respond very defensively when we try to control them. Everyone has a God-given right to freedom of choice, and they resent anyone who tries to take that from them. I finally realized that what I was doing was ungodly, and therefore it was never going to work. Not only would I never have peace because of my behavior, but I was also systematically alienating most of the people I wanted to have a relationship with. Sadly, I wasted a lot of years in this impossible pursuit before I realized that God wanted me to give Him control of every area of my life. When you stop to think about it, He is in control anyway! But our peace comes as we surrender our desire to be in charge and instead trust in Him.

God desires that we use the wonderful tools He has supplied to control ourselves instead of trying to control people and things. He has given us His Word, His Holy Spirit, and a wide variety of good fruit that we can develop. Self-control is actually a fruit of the Spirit-led life (see Gal. 5:22–23). If you have a tendency toward wanting to control the people and circumstances in your life, I want to strongly suggest that you give it up and start controlling yourself instead. This is your opportunity to say, "I am in control."

Although learning to control ourselves requires patience and endurance, it is well worth it in the end. My circumstances have much less control over me now, simply because my first response is usually to work with God in how I am going to respond to the circumstance. *I am in control by being in control of myself.* When your circumstance is unpleasant or even downright painful, exercise self-control. Say something positive like, "This too will pass, and it will work out for my good in the end." Then discipline yourself to put your time into something that will benefit someone else. The best medicine is to do something good in response to the evil coming against you.

> *I am in control by being in control of myself.*

Happiest When Helping

A study on the principle of the Golden Rule was conducted by Bernard Rimland, director of the Institute for Child Behavior Research. Each person involved in the study was asked to list ten people he knew best and to label them as happy or not happy. Then they were to go through the list again and label each one as selfish or unselfish. Rimland found that all the people labeled happy were also labeled unselfish. "The happiest people are those who help others," he concluded. "Do unto others as you would have them do unto you."

God gives us an ability to love others at all times, but this ability is developed only as we exercise it; and we all know that exercise requires discipline and self-control. Start doing the right thing on purpose, rather than merely being a slave to how you feel at the moment.

We don't have to wait to see how we feel about a thing and then respond. We can respond properly no matter how we feel. Do you really want to be a slave all of your life to your emotions? I am sure you don't, but you are the only one who can prevent that from happening.

Discipline might be one of the most misunderstood entities of all time. I don't think I know anyone who breaks into a smile in anticipation of exercising discipline. But the truth is that *discipline is our friend, not our enemy*. It helps us live the life that we will enjoy the

> *Discipline is our friend, not our enemy.*

most when all is said and done. Discipline may not put a smile on our faces while it is in action, but its fruit is a successful and joyful life.

I doubt that it is possible to find a happy and successful person who does not regularly discipline himself. I told you in the beginning that you would need to make decisions as you read this book. No matter what you read or study, it will not help you unless you make decisions. Do you want to be happy and successful? If you do, then discipline is a must, and disciplining the emotions is especially important.

The human personality consists of roughly four-fifths emotions and one-fifth intellect. This means our decisions are made on the basis of 80 percent emotion and 20 percent intellect or reason. It's no wonder that we see so many people make bad decisions! Many of our decisions are good, but if we don't follow through on them, they mean nothing. Emotion may help us get started in the right direction, but it is rarely there at the finish line. Sooner or later we must press forward without the support of emotion and employ discipline.

Translated from the Greek language, the word *discipline* means "saving the mind or to be safe; an admonishment or calling to soundness of mind or to self-control." In other words, a person who is thinking properly with soundness of mind will discipline all areas of her life. I believe our thoughts, words, and emotions are among the most important areas we need to discipline. A disciplined person must maintain the correct mental attitude toward issues that arise. It is much easier to maintain a right attitude than to regain it once it is lost. Don't let that thought pass by without thinking it over. Let me say it again: *It is much easier to maintain a right attitude than to regain it once it is lost.*

God did not give us a spirit of timidity (of cowardice, of craven and cringing and fawning fear), but [He has given us a spirit] of power and of love and of calm and well-balanced mind and discipline and self-control. (2 Timothy 1:7)

We can clearly see from this scripture that God has equipped us with a sound mind, one that stays calm (not emotional), well-balanced, disciplined, and self-controlled. However, we must choose to use our sound minds. Having a thing does no good if we don't use it, and it is almost always painful to start using something that has lain dormant for a long time. When I started working out at the gym and using the muscle I already had, I can assure you it was painful. It stands to reason that if any person has allowed his emotions to have control and has spent most of his life doing what he felt like doing, it will be painful when he begins to exercise discipline. It is always hard to do something we are not accustomed to doing, but if we don't do it, we will be sorry later on.

Dave says, "We can either make ourselves accountable or we will eventually be made accountable by our circumstances." If a person doesn't discipline their spending, they will eventually be made accountable by the debt they have incurred and the pressure and problems it causes. If a person doesn't discipline herself to do what is needed in order to maintain a good marriage, she may end up in a messy divorce with lots of people getting hurt.

Hannah Whitehall Smith, the author of *The Christian's Secret of a Happy Life*, said, "God disciplines the soul by inward exercises and outward providences." What she means is that God will put into our hearts the right thing to do in every situation, but if we choose not to do it, then He will allow our circumstances to become our teacher.

I Want It, and I Am Going to Get It!

Although determination is a great asset and vital to success, it can be very unattractive and dangerous if it is rooted in fleshly, carnal passions rather than in God's will.

The book of Jude mentions three men whose attitude was "I want it, and I am going to get it!" That attitude brought destruction into each of their lives.

> Woe to them! For they have run riotously in the way of Cain, and have abandoned themselves for the sake of gain [it offers them, following] the error of Balaam, and have perished in rebellion [like that] of Korah! *(v. 11)*

Cain, Balaam, and Korah all abandoned themselves to unbridled emotion for the sake of what they thought it would bring them, and their rebellion against God and the wisdom He had placed in them caused them to perish.

Cain wanted the favor that his brother, Abel, had with God, but he didn't want to do what Abel did to get it. Abel had brought his very best offering to God, while Cain brought something, but not his best. God accepted Abel and his offering but not Cain's, and when Cain displayed jeal-ousy and hatred toward his brother, God said, "Sin crouches at your door; its desire is for you, but you must master it" (Gen. 4:7).

Cain didn't deal with his sinful passion and wrong desire, and he rose up and killed his brother. Because he did not dis-cipline his emotions, he would spend the remainder of his life living under a curse. God told him that when he tilled the ground it would not yield its strength; that he would be a fugi-tive and a vagabond on the earth, living in perpetual exile, a degraded outcast. Just stop for a moment and ask yourself whether his unbridled emotions brought him joy and success.

In Numbers 16 we meet Korah, one of 250 men who rose up against Moses, God's chosen man to lead the Israelites into the Promised Land. Apparently, Korah and his associ-ates didn't like the choice that God had made, and they were jealous of Moses' authority. They gathered together against Moses and Aaron, complaining that they were lifting them-selves up above everyone else. In other words, "Moses, we don't like your attitude. Who do you think you are? Don't try to tell us what to do because we are just as important as you are." They missed the entire point, which was that God had put Moses in the job he had, and it was their job to submit to God's choice. Their blessing would have been in their sub-mission, but they listened to their feelings instead of wisdom.

When Moses heard what they said, he began to pray for them, knowing how dangerous their rebellious words were. To make a long story short, God opened a hole in the earth and it swallowed Korah and his men and all they had . . . end of story!

God gave them an opportunity to change their minds and realize how blessed they were to be chosen as leaders, but they still were not satisfied because they wanted what Moses had and were determined they were going to get it. But in the end, they not only did not get what they wanted, but they lost everything they had, including their lives.

Balaam was a prophet or a foreteller of future events. He was a man greatly used by God and one whose advice was sought by many. The king of Moab wanted Balaam to curse the king's enemies so he could defeat them, but Balaam refused. God spoke to Balaam and told him not to curse the people because He had already blessed them. At first Balaam told Moab that he could not comply with his wishes because God had already given him direction. Moab offered gifts and money, hoping to persuade Balaam to change his mind (see Num. 22).

For a while, Balaam persisted in doing what he knew was right. But eventually greed got the best of him, and he went along with King Moab, intending to attempt to go against God. God sent the Angel of the Lord, who used a donkey to pin the great prophet against the wall, crush his foot, and speak to him. How embarrassing it must have been for the so-called great and sought-after man to be corrected by a donkey! Eventually, Balaam's eyes were opened, and he saw the angel who told him that he had been willfully obstinate and contrary toward God. Thankfully, Balaam saw how foolish he was being before it was too late and told King Moab that he had no power at all to say anything except what God told him to say (see Num. 22:38).

If we persist in following unbridled emotion, the result will not be good, but it is never too late to get back on the right path. Cain and Korah did not change and were destroyed, but Balaam made a change before it was too late.

I love learning because it gives me the option of changing what is wrong and doing what is right. Please don't read this book as if it were a nice story about other people. Apply its message to your own life, and don't let emotion rule you.

But It Feels Right!

I think there are levels of feeling, and we need to be able to discern the difference between surface feelings and those things we feel deep in our hearts. There are times when I feel deep in my spirit that God wants me to do or not do a thing, and it is important for me to follow those feelings, but there are other more surface feelings that cause me trouble if I follow them. For instance, I might feel like eating brownies and ice cream every night followed by a huge bowl of salty popcorn, but it will definitely cause trouble. I will gain weight, and I won't feel as energetic as I should. As I mentioned earlier in the book, we are spirits who have souls and bodies. Our spirits are the deepest parts of us, and the place where God makes His home after we receive Jesus Christ as our Savior. Our regenerated spirits become the throne of God and He speaks to us, leading and guiding us from there. There are other feelings we have that are merely emotion and they reside in the soul, a more shallow part of our being. As long as we follow those feelings, we will never get what we truly want out of life, and we will actually make lots of messes that cause trouble for us and for others.

A good example of a person following a surface feeling is found in Genesis 27. In his old age, Isaac had lost his eyesight. He knew that he was going to die soon, and it was time to give the blessing of the firstborn to his elder son, Esau. He had two sons, Esau and Jacob, and his wife, Rebekah, favored Jacob. She wanted him to have the blessing rather than Esau. Since Isaac could not see well, Rebekah hatched a plan to deceive him by making him believe that Jacob was Esau.

Esau was a hairy man, and Jacob had smooth skin. Rebekah placed an animal skin on Jacob's arm and told him to go to his father and pretend to be his brother. When the special meal required for the blessing ceremony was prepared and it was time to give the blessing, Isaac *felt* in his heart that Jacob could not be Esau, but he *felt* his arm and decided it must be Esau because he was hairy. This single instance of following the wrong feelings caused trouble for many years to come.

It caused trouble between the brothers; it caused fear, hiding, dread of being caught, guilt over the deception, and lots of other negative emotions that were all rooted in the one action of following a surface feeling rather than a deeper heart feeling.

Just imagine all the negative results when a married man has an extramarital affair because of feelings he experienced toward another woman. Or think of the years that so many spend in prison because they followed feelings of rage or anger and murdered someone, even though they knew deep inside it was wrong.

There are times when something may feel right, but it is wise to check to see where the feeling is coming from. Is it just an emotional feeling or is it something you truly feel in your heart is right?

It Feels Like God's Will

How can we know the will of God? This is perhaps one of the most important issues for Christians who want to obey God. Surely Isaac would not have purposely disobeyed God, but because he followed his feelings without putting them to the test, he did.

"I just felt this is what God wanted me to do" can be a lame excuse for self-will, but the sincere Christian will test the impression he has received to examine its validity.

First Thessalonians 5:21 states that we should test everything and hold on to what is good. Satan often appears as an angel of light. He will even whisper Scripture to us to confirm something we want to do, if doing it will get us into trouble. We can make the Bible say almost anything by taking bits and pieces of it, but if we examine all of Scripture as a whole, it will protect our path.

Martin liked cars. In fact, he was obsessed with having a new one every year. He enjoyed the whole experience of shopping for the car, test-driving the car, bargaining with the salesman, driving it off the car lot, washing and polishing it in his driveway, and having the neighbors come over to admire it. When Martin went out to buy his new car for the current year, his wife was set against it. She felt that they needed to get out of debt instead of incurring more debt. Martin told her that he would pray about it and would not do it unless he felt that God approved. Martin was sincere about hearing from God, but he also had a very strong desire for the car. As he prayed and waited on God, he opened his Bible and his eyes rested on Psalm 67:6, which reads, "The earth has yielded its harvest [in evidence of God's approval]; God, even our own God, will bless us."

Martin decided that getting the car he wanted was his harvest for working hard during the past year and that it was God's way of blessing him. It is a good scripture, and certainly Martin could have received it as approval to get the car, except God's Word also teaches us to get out of debt and that the borrower is a servant to the lender. God's Word warns against greed and overusing the things of this world. Martin's decision was going to cause strife with his wife, and the car he already had was a perfectly wonderful car. The payment on the new car was going to be $150 a month more than his current payment, and it was going to create the need for financial adjustments that Martin had decided could come from the family clothing allowance. In other words he was being selfish, which the Bible clearly teaches against.

In this instance Martin used Scripture to get his own way without honestly looking at the whole counsel of God's Word.

In James Dobson's book *Emotions: Can You Trust Them?* he draws on the wisdom of Martin Wells Knapp, who in his 1892 book *Impressions* suggested four simple questions that could be used to test our urges and impressions. I've paraphrased Knapp's questions below and applied them to Martin's desire for a new car:

1. Is what you want to do scriptural? Is it in harmony with the entire Bible?

2. Is it right when examined by morality and decency? Certainly the purchase of an automobile is not morally wrong or indecent, but Martin's selfish behavior was not right.

3. Is God's providence opening the door for what we desire, or are we kicking the door down? If God had suddenly provided an additional $150 per month in income, or if the car dealership had offered to take Martin's current car in trade and assured him the payment would be no higher than his current one, then he might have rightly concluded that God was opening the door for him to have the car. As it was, though, Martin had none of those providential signs.

4. Is it reasonable? Was it even common sense for Martin to feel he must have a new automobile every year, even though his family would need to sacrifice for him to do so? Was his decision going to build good family relationships and teach his children how to manage their finances properly as they grew into adulthood? Was his decision consistent with the character of God?

We can easily see that if Martin had submitted his desire to a scriptural test, he would have known that purchasing the new car at that time was incorrect. As humans we sadly fall into this pit of doing what we want to do and then saying we felt it was God urging on our actions. God does speak to His people and promises to lead and guide us, but it is dangerous to blindly follow every impression one receives.

I Feel Excited About This!

Excitement is a good feeling; we all enjoy it. Sometimes we need the fuel of excitement to help us enjoy a thing, but at other times if we make serious decisions based on excitement alone, it can cause trouble.

Excitement might be referred to as impulse that is a sudden urge to do a thing. The Bible tells us that catering to impulse is a sign of spiritual immaturity and is not pleasing to God (see Rom. 8:8, 1 Cor. 3:1–3). If we took the time to examine some of our feelings, we would find them to be very irrational.

For example, people often commit to things that are actually impossible for them to do. They commit in excitement or due to an impulse without taking the time to consider whether they will be able to finish what they started. If we are honest, we have to admit that we create a lot of the messes in our lives ourselves. We may blame them on other things and people, but truly much of it is our own fault.

Have you ever done anything impulsively and been very sorry later but had no way to undo what you had done? I know I have, and I don't think there is a worse feeling in the world for me. I know the trouble that can be caused by following sudden urges without examining them wisely.

Feelings are very fickle. They are always changing; they come and go like the waves in the ocean. They are up, then down, and seem to be controlled by some unseen force that we don't understand. "Why do I feel the way I feel?" is a frequently asked question, but our confusion is often like what someone with no scientific knowledge might feel trying to understand why sometimes the ocean is smooth and flat and at other times it is thrashing about wildly. It just is, and we accept that.

If we are wise, we don't go sailing in the ocean when it is wild with waves that appear dangerous, and neither should we get into our emotions when they are wildly changing; first up and then down, here and there, coming and going. The best thing to do is wait for them to settle before taking any action. Take the helm and sail your own ship. Don't just get into the boat with nobody at the helm and merely hope that the waves of life take you somewhere good.

> *Don't just get into the boat with nobody at the helm and merely hope that the waves of life take you somewhere good.*

Decision and confession: *I will control how I respond to every situation.*

PART II

In the next several chapters, I'll be addressing emotions that give us particular trouble, including anger, guilt, bitterness and resentment, depression, and discouragement. As you read, it is very important that you understand—and believe—that *you can control* these unpleasant emotions. If you don't, these troubling emotions will end up controlling you and your life. The reason you can control them is because God has supplied you with what you need to do so. We cannot do anything without His help, but that is always available for anyone who will humble herself and ask for it.

CHAPTER
11

Anger

The three most harmful negative emotions are anger, guilt, and fear. And anger is number one. It is also the strongest and most dangerous of all passions. When a crime is described as being one of passion, that means it was fueled by anger. Anger is such a dangerous emotion that people end up in prison because of what it causes them to do! While we need to take everything the Bible teaches very seriously, clearly it's important to pay special attention to what God tells us about anger and how to handle it.

Anger manifests itself in different ways. One type of anger is characterized by quickly blazing up and then subsiding just as quickly. Another type tends to settle in and take root; like a low-grade virus, it lingers in the mind and waits for the perfect opportunity to take revenge. Another type of anger provokes us to take quick action. Anger can manifest in yelling, hitting, damaging, or otherwise bringing harm to its focus. Anger criticizes, withdraws, ridicules, humiliates, despises, teases, and puts down; it disrespects, rebels, and may even turn around and take on the role of victim. Some people bury their anger, but like a volcano, anger can stay under the surface for only so long. One way or another, it will emerge.

Some people become irritated by the slightest inconvenience, while others seem to stay calm no matter what happens. These differences are due partly to the temperament we each are born with and partly to the circumstances we encounter in the early years of our lives while our personalities are being formed.

Although we cannot use "personality type" as an excuse for a bad temper, it is wise to realize that different people do handle conflict differently. Dave rarely gets upset about anything (except while he's driving). If he encounters a really grouchy waitress or clerk, instead of getting angry because they are rude to him, he teases them and tries to get them in a good mood. But if someone is rude to me, I'm more likely to feel anger rising and be tempted to tell them what I think of their behavior. That is exactly what I did for years until I learned how to manage my emotions. I'm not always successful, but at least I succeed more than I fail, and the good news is that I am still growing.

I've often thought it unfair that I have to work so hard at controlling myself, while for Dave, control seems to come naturally. But we all have strengths and weaknesses in different areas. Complaining about our differences doesn't change them. You have to play the hand you are dealt. Take what you have and do the best you can with it.

Is Anger a Sin?

Many Christians are confused about anger. They think that as godly individuals they should never get angry. They wonder why they keep having to deal with anger when it's something they don't want to feel. Anger can be an involuntary response whether we want to feel it or not. A person with damaged emotions from past trauma or abuse may, and probably will, respond in a self-protective mode and display anger more easily than someone who was never mistreated. Thankfully, through God's help those damaged emotions can be healed, and we can learn to have more balanced and reasonable responses to people, things, and situations.

Not all anger is a sin, but some of it is. The Bible speaks of a righteous anger that even God Himself has. It is anger against sin, injustice, rebellion, pettiness, and other such things.

God's Word says, "When angry, do not sin" (Eph. 4:26); and Proverbs 16:32 says, "He who is slow to anger is better than the mighty, he who rules his [own] spirit than he who takes a city." I recall one morning as I was preparing to go to preach, Dave and I got into an argument. I was studying and he said something to me that made me blaze up quickly with anger. We said some unkind words to each other and then he left for work. I continued to think angry thoughts and have angry feelings. Then my anger turned into guilt and I started thinking, *How can I possibly go to church and tell others how to conduct their lives according to Scripture if I cannot control my anger?* The feelings of guilt not only continued but they intensified. As the pressure mounted, I started to feel almost frantic when suddenly I heard God whisper in my heart, *Anger is not a sin; it is what you do with it that becomes sin.* That was one of the first lessons God gave me in understanding that emotions cannot be expected to merely go away because we have become Christians, but rather we are to learn how to manage them.

Ephesians goes on to say, "Do not ever let your wrath (your exasperation, your fury or indignation) last until the sun goes down" (4:26). When we do hold on to anger, it gives the devil a foothold in our lives (see v. 27). This scripture has been life-changing for me by helping me learn more about emotions and what to do with them.

Sinful Anger

What is the difference between apparently innocent emotions that are just a part of life and emotions that are sinful? Unacceptable and sinful anger is that which motivates us to hurt our fellow human being. When we want to lash out vengefully and inflict pain on others, we are definitely out of God's will. Not even the injustice of others gives us the right to inflict pain on them. God says clearly that vengeance is His, and our position is to be one of faith in Him, waiting patiently and lovingly as He works justice in our lives. When Jesus was about to be captured prior to His crucifixion, Peter took out his sword and cut off a soldier's ear. Jesus rebuked him and healed the man's ear. Peter seemed to be justified in his actions, but Jesus condemned his behavior.

Peter was given to fits of temper and was rather emotional, so anger was his natural response to things he did not like or did not feel were right. Even a short study of the life of Peter reveals his emotional nature, but God allowed him to see his own shortcomings and the problems they caused and Peter was eventually changed.

Moses lost a privilege he had looked forward to for years due to uncontrolled anger. In Numbers 20:1–12 we see that he reacted emotionally in anger toward the Israelites one time too many, and God told him he would not be permitted to take them into the Promised Land.

I can understand Moses' anger, because leading the Israelites through the wilderness and listening to incessant complaining would have made me angry too. But to whom much is given, much is required. Moses was given a privilege above other men, and he was expected to manage his emotions.

Controlling the passion of anger, especially if you have an aggressive and outspoken nature, can be one of the more challenging things you will face in life, but controlling it is certainly possible with God's help. Remember that a man who controls his anger is said to be strong enough to conquer an entire city (see Prov. 16:32).

Will you make a decision not to let anger control you and your actions?

Hatred

Nothing justifies an attitude of hatred. I admit that I hated my father passionately for many, many years. That hatred

did not change my father or make him pay for his wrongdoing, but it did poison me. It took away my peace and my
joy, and my sin of hatred separated me from the intimate
presence of God.

First John 4:20 reads: "He who does not love his brother,
whom he has seen, cannot love God, Whom he has not seen."
We cannot maintain love for God and hatred for man in our
heart at the same time. When God tells us to forgive our enemies, it is for our own benefit.

We may have been cruelly treated and have every reason
to hate someone, but we have no right to. No one was more
unjustly treated than Jesus, and yet He asked God to forgive
His tormentors, saying they did not know what they were
doing (see Luke 23:34). The Bible says they hated Jesus without a cause (see John 15:25). That has always seemed very
sad to me. He came for only one purpose, and that was to
help and bless humankind, and they hated Him because He
was good and they were evil.

John tells us that hatred in our hearts is equivalent to murder (see 1 John 3:15).

Righteous Anger

The Bible speaks of righteous anger, which is anger against
all sin and everything that offends God. Abuse and injustice
of all kinds make me angry. I get angry at the devil when I
see children starving in India, Asia, Africa, and other places
I have traveled to for mission outreaches.

Even God has righteous anger! God got angry when He

saw the hardness of His people's hearts (see Mark 3:5). Thankfully, His anger is for a moment, but His favor is for a lifetime (see Psalm 30:5). Even though God is slow to anger, I am sure there are many injustices in this world that do make Him angry. I am certainly glad He manages His emotions, aren't you?

Although righteous anger is not a sin, what we do with it can become sin. I am very angry at the devil, but I have discovered that the only way to get him back for the evil he does is by doing good myself. Good is the one thing that Satan, the personification of evil, cannot stand. I always say, "If you want to give the devil a nervous breakdown, just get up every day and see how much good you can do."

Uncontrolled anger, even righteous anger, can quickly turn into rage, and that is dangerous. For example, people who are angry concerning abortion laws, or prayer being taken out of school, or the loss of Christian rights that is prevalent today feel righteous anger, but even that can be displayed improperly. We are all aware of Christians who have done great harm to others because of uncontrolled rage over an injustice. But remember, we are to speak the truth in love, not in rage. That doesn't mean we can't be strong as we speak out against injustice, but any lack of control will only open a door for the devil—and this is particularly true when it comes to anger. We must remember—and obey—what the Bible says: "Don't let the sun set on your anger!" (see Eph. 4:26).

Repressed Anger

Anger that is expressed inappropriately is a problem, but so is repressed anger. Anger that is stuffed inside and not dealt with properly will eventually come out one way or another. It may show up in depression, anxiety, rage, or any of a variety of other negative emotions—but it *will* come out. It can even manifest in sickness and disease. If we don't deal with our anger quickly, we will eventually either explode or implode.

> *If we don't deal with our anger quickly, we will eventually either explode or implode.*

The right way to express anger is to talk to God. Tell Him all about the way you feel and ask Him to help you manage the feelings properly. We have not because we ask not! (See James 4:2.) Talk to a professional or a mature friend if necessary, but do not pretend you're not angry when you are. That's not managing your emotions—that is ignoring them, and it is dangerous.

One thing that helps me deal properly with anger is to realize that sometimes God permits people to irritate me in order to help me grow in patience and unconditional love. None of the fruit of the Spirit develops without something to make us exercise them. Ouch! I wish I could magically have all these wonderful fruit working full force in my life without any effort on my part, but that is just not the way it works. The offending person's bad behavior is not right, but God often uses them as sandpaper in our lives, to polish our rough edges. He is more concerned about changing our characters than He is about changing our circumstances to make them all comfortable for us. God promises deliverance if we trust Him, but the timing is in His hands.

If I get angry when someone does something to me that's wrong, is my anger any less wrong than the wrong they committed? I think not. Sometimes their wrongdoing merely exposes my weakness and I am able to repent and ask God to help me overcome it. Be determined to get something good out of every trial you face in life, and don't ever let the sun go down on your anger.

This is a good time to ask yourself if you are angry about anything or at anyone, and if your answer is yes, then you can begin controlling that emotion right now.

Some of the explosive people we encounter in life are actually people who are full of anger over something they have buried and refused to deal with. Even they may not understand why they feel so angry all the time. They are like time bombs ticking away, just waiting for someone or something to set them off. They explode at the slightest provocation, and quite often their anger seems extreme for the situation they are dealing with.

Melody's mother was mentally ill, and she frequently locked her in the closet for punishment. Some days she spent more time in the dark closet than she did in the house. This abuse left Melody very angry, but not knowing how to deal with her anger, she simply left home when she was old enough to do so and tried to forget the whole thing. That sounds good; after all, we are instructed in God's Word to let go of what lies behind. However, that does not mean to avoid dealing with it. Melody married at the age of nineteen because she was desperate to experience love, and she and her husband had three children within the first five years of their rather rocky relationship.

Melody was moody. She was either depressed or angry most of the time, and it seemed that everyone had to walk on eggshells, so to speak, to prevent setting her off. The atmosphere in the house was very tense. Melody frequently overreacted to minor situations. At dinner one evening, her daughter Katie, who was three years old, accidentally spilled her glass of milk at the table. Melody got up and threw her chair across the room as she ranted and raved on and on about how nobody in the house seemed to be able to do anything right. The meal was ruined for everyone. Her husband, James, left the house to prevent starting an argument with her and making things even worse, and the children sat at the table with fearful looks on their faces, crying and wondering what Mama would do next.

Melody was always sorry shortly after her explosions, and she tried to make up for her bad behavior by doing something nice for the children, but the guilt she felt because she could not control herself was almost overwhelming. She didn't know what to do, so she did nothing. Eventually, her depression became so bad that she was advised to see a psychiatrist. Thankfully, the one she went to was a Christian in addition to being a great counselor, and he was able to help Melody see that deep down inside she was still very angry about the way her mother had treated her, and this was causing all her emotional problems. He helped her face the truth, forgive her mother, and learn how to control her emotions.

Melody's story ended well, but there are hundreds of

thousands of people in the world like Melody who are emotional time bombs just waiting to explode. Sadly, they may spend their entire lives being miserable and ruining relationships because they never deal with the root of their problem.

Although there are very serious situations like Melody's that require a lot of time to heal, there are also things we deal with daily. Each day we may have an opportunity to be offended or to not take the offense. Some psychologists teach that we need to express all our anger, but according to God's Word, there are many things that we need to just let go of.

One teacher wrote the following on her classroom blackboard: "Hatred is stored-up anger; therefore, it is a loving thing to get mad." That is a ridiculous thing to teach children. It would be much better to teach them to forgive. Surely the types of offenses the children were dealing with daily did not warrant a "let your anger come out session." Some psychologists tell people when they are angry to pound on a table or hit something until they feel they have released their anger. I don't see any such suggestions in the Bible, and I think if I pounded a table when I was angry, all I would get would be a sore hand. If these are the types of things we are learning and teaching our children, it is not surprising that our society is so dangerous today. It is sad indeed when we have to offer special classes to teach people how to handle road rage! Or when we have to fear that someone may walk up and shoot us because they are angry about the way their life has gone.

Since God's Word tells us not to let the sun set on our anger, surely God expects us simply to let some things go. As we navigate life, we will need to be generous in mercy in order not to be angry most of the time. In the Amplified Bible we learn that to forgive means to "let it drop (leave it, let it go)" (Mark 11:25). That plan sounds pretty good to me. We must learn to choose our battles wisely in life because there are far too many to fight them all. Sometimes God still says, as He did to the Israelites, "The battle is not yours, but God's" (2 Chron. 20:15).

How can you know when to express anger and when to just let it go? I can only tell you what works for me. My first line of defense is to give it to God—to simply let it go and trust Him to do what is right. If the issue keeps bothering me for more than a few days, I will talk to Dave or perhaps one of my children in the hope that just getting it out in the open will bring release. I don't talk to them in a spirit of gossip or criticism, but I do it to get the help that I need. Sometimes another person can offer a different perspective on the situation that I am not seeing. If none of that works, then I start seeking God about whether or not He wants me to confront the person who has angered me. If I feel that He does, then I do it.

Sometimes it is best for the other person if you confront them, but I always want to make sure I am doing it for their good and not my carnal need to tell them off or try to change them. Rather, I express anger properly or give it to God. I am not repressing it. I have let it go and it is not festering in me, causing infection and damage to my soul.

When someone mistreats me, I initially feel angry, then I spend the next few minutes or hours, depending on the seriousness of the mistreatment, getting the emotion under control. I talk to myself and tell myself how foolish it is to let some unkind person ruin my day. I follow Scripture and pray for the person who hurt me. I try to believe the best of the person who offended me and try to get my mind off the offense and onto something more pleasant. I find within a short period of time the emotion is calming down. Obeying and meditating on the Word of God is medicine for our souls. It brings not only instruction but comfort in every situation.

As you can see, there are several ways we can deal with anger, but remember that we can't express it in an unloving way, we can't repress it, and we can't ignore it. Anger is a real emotion, and we have to deal with it one way or another.

Perception or Reality?

Have you ever heard the statement "Perception is reality"? If we perceive that we're in jeopardy, then whether or not it's actually true, we behave as if it's true. And our behavior shapes the quality of our lives. We've all heard about people who lived like paupers, living out their final years without decent food, clothing, and shelter because they were worried about finances. Then after their deaths, it's discovered that they were actually rich, sometimes with millions of dollars in savings accounts!

They lived in fear and desperation when they could have lived in luxury. They believed they were poor and lived accordingly.

How we perceive things is how we see them. In my child-hood, I suffered abuse that made me feel the need to defend myself from emotional and physical attack. Because of that conditioning, those feelings and responses remained for many years into my adulthood. I frequently perceived that I was being attacked and needed to defend myself. But my life had changed! I married Dave, who is my biggest supporter and cheerleader. Imagine my surprise when he asked me one morning why I acted as if he were my enemy!

It took a long time for me to let the Holy Spirit work with me and teach me to judge things through the eyes of God, not the eyes of an abusive world. On that particular morning, Dave had expressed disagreement with me about something, and I received it as rejection. My anger flared and words began to fly. In those days I still had a shame-based nature and felt so bad about myself that if anyone disagreed with me or tried to correct me about anything, I always got upset.

I spent many years in confusion about anger because I didn't understand the root of my problem. I would find myself angry and argumentative when I had initially intended to have a very simple discussion about something. Satan had a foothold in my life, and I needed revelation from God in order to see clearly. He taught me that I had a root of rejection in my life that manifested in anger, and that when people disagreed with my opinion, I took it personally as if they were rejecting me. I did not yet know how to separate my "who" from my "do." If people didn't agree with everything I did or said, I felt they were rejecting me.

I was preparing to go teach God's Word that morning, and Satan saw an opportunity to create a disturbance by taking advantage of my weakness. He managed to start an argument between Dave and me, knowing it would leave me feeling guilty and condemned and prevent me from teaching God's

Word with confidence. But God came to my rescue! He showed me that the anger I felt just needed to be managed. I repented for the argument, called Dave and apologized, and went on to my meeting with peace.

Over the years, as God healed me from my past pain, I gradually felt less and less anger. But while He was healing me, God taught me that my anger was not sin if I controlled it. My emotions were damaged, and I often reacted the way a wounded animal would. Today, I rarely feel angry unless the threat or attack toward me is genuine.

God has given us the emotion of anger to let us know when we are being mistreated; kept under control, it is a good thing.

> *When angry, count to ten before you speak; if very angry, count to one hundred.*
> Horace

When angry, count to ten before you speak;
if very angry, count to one hundred.
Horace

Is It Always Going to Be So Difficult to Manage My Emotions?

Maybe you're thinking, *I have so many strong emotions; how am I going to manage them all?* I have found that God usually deals with me one issue at a time. By reading this book you are gaining an overall understanding of emotions and, hopefully, why you feel the way you feel at times. You are learning that you must first and foremost depend on God, then take action and be aggressive in your determination not to be a slave to your feelings. I frequently remind people that nothing changes just because you read a book. It's what you do with the knowledge you gain from reading the book that will lead to change.

I realize that change is not always easy, and perhaps there will be times when you think, *I just don't know if I will ever get this right.* But I assure you that if you will not give up, you will keep making progress, and eventually you will have many of your emotions trained and they simply will not be unruly. They will respond the same way a child does when we train them properly. The more we refuse to let our negative emotions rule us, the weaker they become, and eventually we just need to do daily maintenance.

I am not saying that you will never feel angry again, but the anger you do feel will be much easier to manage than it has been in the past. I can honestly say that twenty years ago I was very emotional and now I am very stable. I know from experience that the principles I am sharing with you will work wonderfully in your life if you diligently apply them. Always remember that gaining a victory is more difficult than maintaining it once you have it.

Decision and confession: *I will not live as an angry person. I will deal with anger in a godly way.*

CHAPTER

12

Guilt

Guilt is a sense of responsibility concerning something negative that has befallen others or yourself. It is a feeling of regret over some action taken or not taken. Guilt is a terrible feeling to bear. We are not built for guilt, and it damages our souls and personalities—even our health. Guilt steals our peace and joy. It can become a prison without a key.

Guilt leaves us with a sense of obligation to make up in some way for the wrong we did or imagine we did. The burden of guilt coupled with a desire to pay for our crimes is a miserable life indeed. I know a woman who spent hundreds of thousands of dollars in treatment programs and found no help until she received Jesus as her Savior and believed that He paid the debt she owed when He died on the cross. The gospel of Jesus Christ is good news indeed! Because we could not, He paid, and now there is no condemnation or guilt for those who are in Christ (see Rom. 8:1).

We don't ignore our sins, but instead we face them boldly;

we confess them (telling all) and receive God's amazing forgiveness.

> I acknowledged my sin to You, and my iniquity I did not hide. I said, I will confess my transgressions to the Lord [continually unfolding the past till all is told]—then You [instantly] forgave me the guilt and iniquity of my sin. Selah [pause, and calmly think of that]!   *(Psalm 32:5)*

Let's do what the Scripture suggests. Let's pause and calmly think of what the verse is saying. If we acknowledge (admit) our sin to God and tell all, refusing to hide our sin, God will instantly forgive us and remove the guilt. If the sin is gone, there is nothing to feel guilty about. The feeling of guilt does not always go away instantly, but we can take God at His word and say with Him, "I am forgiven, and the guilt has been removed." I have discovered that my feelings will eventually catch up with my decision, but if I let my feelings make my decisions, I will always be a slave to them.

I know of a woman who was a real warrior for the Lord. She taught Sunday school, visited women in the local prison on Friday nights, volunteered to clean the church sanctuary on Saturdays, and tithed regularly. She raised two daughters who became committed Christians and led hundreds of people to the Lord over her lifetime. When she died, grown men came to her funeral and cried. They told her daughters how their mother had given their wives food and money when they themselves had squandered their paychecks.

Only her daughters knew that their mother was one of the unhappiest women in the world. Despite her strong faith, she had committed sins in her youth that haunted her throughout her life. While God had forgiven her, she couldn't forgive herself.

She was stuck in condemnation.

I think stories like this one are some of the saddest in the world. I am sure the woman in the story told others of the love and mercy of God, yet she never truly received it for herself. Perhaps she never understood that she was much more than what she felt. She felt guilty, and so she assumed she was guilty and let it steal her joy. This story is repeated in multiplied millions of lives and is one of the reasons I am writing this book. *We can live by the truth in God's Word and not the way we feel.*

We can live by the truth in God's Word and not the way we feel.

Condemnation and Conviction

We must learn the difference between condemnation (guilt) and true conviction from God that we have done something wrong. Condemnation presses us down and manifests as a heavy burden that requires us to pay for our errors. Conviction is the work of the Holy Spirit, who is showing us that we have sinned and inviting us to confess our sins, to receive forgiveness and God's help to improve our behavior in the future. Condemnation makes the problem worse; conviction is intended to lift us out of it. The result of each is entirely different from the other.

When you feel guilty, the first thing to do is ask yourself if you are guilty according to God's Word. Perhaps you are.

If so, confess your sin to God; turn away from that sin and don't repeat it. If you need to apologize to the person you have wronged, do it. Then... forgive yourself and let go of it! God already did, and if you refuse to, then you'll miss out on the joy of redemption that God wants us all to experience.

Sometimes you may well find that you are not guilty according to God's Word. For example, I can recall feeling guilty when I tried to rest. For years I drove myself incessantly to work, work, work because I felt good when I was accomplishing something and felt guilty if I was enjoying myself. I finally came to a crisis point and cried out to God about why I couldn't enjoy resting, and He showed me that the guilty feelings were leftovers from my past. My father seemed to approve of me more when I was working and he did not value enjoyment of any kind, so I learned early in life that work is applauded but rest had little or no value.

That thinking is totally wrong according to God's Word. Even He rested from His work of creation and has invited us to enter His rest. The guilt I felt when I tried to rest was unscriptural, irrational, and downright ridiculous. When I stopped believing my feelings alone and started truly examining them in the light of God's Word, I uncovered a huge deception in my life.

What makes you feel guilty? What does God's Word say about the situation? You may discover that yours is a false guilt or it may be real, but either way, the Word of God holds the answer to your dilemma. If it is a false sense of guilt, then declare it to be so and be determined not to let your feelings rule you. If your guilt is based on a real sin, then follow the scriptural pattern for getting rid of it. Repent, tell all, ask for forgiveness, and receive forgiveness by faith. Now believe and confess that your sin, and the guilt, has been taken care of by Jesus. And move on!

The Holy Spirit is given to us for many reasons, and one of the really important ones is to convict us of sin. We should love and appreciate all conviction because without it we could easily live lives of self-deception. A spiritually mature person can receive conviction and not let it condemn them. Correction from God is never rejection. It is a sign of His love that He is unwilling to leave us as we are, but He works daily to change us into His image and help us develop His character.

Real and Imagined Guilt

When you are prone to guilt, the devil has a field day. I guarantee you that he will definitely take advantage of you by working through others to play on your guilt. They may make you feel that they'll suffer greatly if you don't do as they ask. Your response must be to follow your own intuition from God and not take responsibility for their joy. You may have elderly parents who will make you feel guilty if you don't cater to their every whim. We do have a biblical duty to our parents to be sure they are taken care of in their old age, but we cannot be responsible for their joy. Many of the things people expect are *their* expectations, and they can be quite unrealistic. They may be thinking only of themselves without having any understanding of you and your other responsibilities.

The sense of guilt is so awful that we usually will do

almost anything to alleviate it. If we allow others to make us feel guilty, they soon learn how to manipulate us by using our weakness to get what they want. You must understand that you are not obligated to do a thing just because someone else wants you to or thinks that you should. This does not mean we don't want to please people and do what is for their benefit, but we cannot let their desires rule us.

Guilt can be from a real or imagined misdeed. I felt guilty about the abuse in my childhood even though I was not the perpetrator and hated what was being done to me. That guilt developed into what I call an addictive guilt. I just felt guilty all the time over nothing in particular as well as mistakes I did make. I had a false sense of guilt that was rooted in shame.

Emotions have a mind of their own, and Satan uses them to deceive us. We cannot assume because we feel a certain way that those feelings are telling us the truth. In other words, just because I feel guilty does not mean I am guilty. Likewise, I may not feel guilty and yet I have committed sin. I may have reasoned in my mind that what I did was justifiable even though it was against God's Word, and by doing so I deceived myself. The apostle Paul said that he didn't feel anything against himself, but that he was not justified by his feelings. He left everything to God and expected that God would convict him of sin when needed: "I am not conscious of anything against myself, and I feel blameless; but I am not vindicated and acquitted before God on that account. It is the Lord [Himself] Who examines and judges me" (1 Cor. 4:4).

Men who batter their wives make them feel as if the battering is their fault. The women who allow such treatment have little or no self-worth. They feel that if the marriage fails it will be their fault, and many of them actually believe they must deserve the treatment they get. I have heard that 7 percent of all women are physically abused, and 37 percent are verbally or emotionally abused. That means there are a lot of women who feel guilty and have no self-esteem.

Guilt and Anger

Guilt is one of the root causes of anger. We inherently know that we are not built for guilt. We may not consciously realize it, but our system rebels against it. God wants us to feel loved and accepted, and for that reason we are told again and again in His Word that He loves us unconditionally. Even when we were still in our sin and before we cared about God at all or even attempted to do anything right, He loved us and sent His Son to die for us and pay for our sins.

When we receive Jesus as our Savior, He takes our sin and gives us His righteousness (see 2 Cor. 5:21). I doubt that many of us understand the full impact of that. At no price to us, we are made right with God. We can feel right instead of wrong!

Why not take a step of faith and try it? Say or think something good about yourself. I am not encouraging a wrong kind of pride, but I am encouraging you to be bold enough to believe you are the wonderful person God says you are.

In Psalm 139, David confessed that he knew God had made him and then said, "Wonderful are Your works, and that my inner self knows right well" (v. 14). Do you believe in your heart that God carefully created you and that you are wonderful? Most people would be afraid to believe that. Why are we more comfortable feeling bad about ourselves than feeling good? Is it because we focus on our faults and rarely even glance at our strengths? We punish ourselves for our failures, but rarely celebrate our victories.

The Song of Solomon is an allegory of the love story between God and His people. Look closely at the following scripture:

> [He exclaimed] O my love, how beautiful you are! There is no flaw in you!   (4:7)

God loves you and sees the good in you. He sees what you are becoming and will be and is not overly concerned about your faults. He knew all of them when He invited you to be in an intimate relationship with Him. All He wants is your love and a willingness to grow in Him.

Your presence is a present to the world. You are unique and one of a kind. Do not ever forget, for even a day... how very special you are!

Your presence is a present to the world. You are unique and one of a kind. *Do not ever forget, for even a day... how very special you are!*

Take a Step of Faith

Will you take a step of faith and no matter how you feel, agree with God that He loves you? You are wonderfully made and have many talents and strengths. You are valuable, and as a believer in Jesus, you are the righteousness of God in Him. You have rightness before God instead of wrongness!

Begin to speak out against feelings of guilt and say, "I am forgiven; therefore, I am not guilty. I am right with God." I think I shared earlier that we believe more of what we hear ourselves say than what others say, so start saying something good and drown out the other voices that condemn you.

Fight for yourself! Fight the good fight of faith and refuse to live below the level at which Jesus wants you to live. His kingdom is righteousness, peace, and joy (see Rom. 14:17). Don't settle for anything less.

Guilt is anger directed at ourselves. Will you stop the destructive cycle, take a step of faith, and declare, "Jesus bore my iniquities and guilt—and I am free!"?

An actress who is very well known has said that she doesn't believe in guilt; she believes in living by impulse as long as what she does causes no harm to others. She has said, "I am free." This woman is living for herself and doing exactly as she pleases, but she appears to be very miserable. Although she is a success on the screen, she is not a true success. Her idea is a very worldly one that is born out of selfishness and is entirely different from what I am talking about. When we say, "I am free," we mean that our freedom was purchased by the blood and sacrifice of Jesus Christ. We live without guilt because He paid for our sins. Without this knowledge there is no true guilt-free living. People may say they are free to do whatever they want, but a truly free person is free to live in obedience to God, and to refrain from doing what they want to do if they know their actions will damage someone else.

From Agony to Ecstasy

We can learn to control guilt by knowing the truth of God's Word and looking at some of the things we feel guilty about in a rational way. It is normal and healthy to feel guilty when we do something wrong, but when it continues and becomes addictive, we have a serious problem that will not go away without confrontation.

Christianity is not a passive religion. God has given us His promises, but we must do our part. We are partners with Him. We believe and He works! We must say and mean it: "I will not be a slave to the emotion of guilt." Study God's Word on the subject of righteousness until you have revelation concerning who you are in Christ.

Our confidence is in Him, not in ourselves, our looks, our educations, our job titles, our social groups, or any other earthly thing. Our worth and value are in the fact that Jesus died for us. God saw you as being valuable so He gave His best. He gave His only Son to purchase your freedom from the bondage of sin and guilt.

Karla Faye Tucker had plenty to feel guilty about. In the wee hours of June 13, 1983, she and her boyfriend, high on drugs, decided to go "visit" Jerry Dean, an acquaintance who Karla felt had wronged her. Dean was home asleep in bed, a woman he'd met that day sleeping by his side.

Tucker and her boyfriend entered the house and surprised the sleeping couple. She struck Dean with a pickax twenty-eight times and then proceeded to execute his companion. Tucker was tried, convicted, and given the death penalty. She lived on death row in the Huntsville, Texas, federal prison for the next fourteen years.

But that's just the beginning of the story.

Her case attracted worldwide attention, partly because she was the first woman to be executed in the United States since before the Civil War. The other reason her case was covered widely was because Tucker had become a Christian while she was in prison, and none other than Pat Robertson and Pope John Paul had learned of her extraordinary work with others during her years of imprisonment. They both issued pleas to the governor to spare her.

On February 3, 1998, Tucker was taken to the room where she would die by lethal injection. In her final moments, she said, "I would like to say to the Thornton family and Jerry Dean's family that I am so sorry...I'm going to be face-to-face with Jesus now. I love you all very much. I will see you all when you get there. I will wait for you." According to witnesses, she appeared to be humming softly as she waited to meet her Lord.

Karla Faye Tucker was very guilty. She was guilty of acts that are hard to even contemplate. She was also redeemed from her guilt by God when she accepted Christ, and she knew that. She could have spent her prison term focusing on her guilt. Instead, she spent her remaining years teaching Bible study groups, helping other inmates, and praising the Lord for His mercy.

If an ax murderer can acknowledge her guilt, accept God's forgiveness, and move on, then so can you and I. While my own situation is far less dramatic than Karla Faye Tucker's, I had a huge problem with feelings of guilt. I had to fight a real battle to finally be able to say, "I am free." If I can do it, so can you. If anyone can be free, you can be free, so don't settle for anything less. Living without the constant companion of guilt is ecstasy; it is wonderful and it is available to all who will believe.

Living Guilt-Free

I heard a story about a man who had been cheating on his income taxes for a few years. He began to feel guilty, and eventually the guilt was preventing him from sleeping well. He wrote the IRS a letter and told them he had been cheating on his income taxes and that he had enclosed a check for $150. He further stated that if he still did not sleep well, he would send more money later.

Don't just do enough of what is right to ease feelings of guilt, but instead make a decision that you are going to learn to live guilt-free. There are two ways to do that. The first and best way is to choose the right thing in the first place and then there is no reason to feel guilty. Or, immediately ask for God's forgiveness when you recognize that you have sinned. Don't be satisfied with merely fighting guilt every day, but instead study God's Word and pray about it until you can genuinely say, "There is no condemnation for those who are in Christ" (see Rom. 8:1).

Decision and confession: *I will not waste my life feeling guilty.*

CHAPTER
13

Fear

Fear is an emotion that we often experience. Some fear is healthy and keeps us out of trouble. The fear of stepping out into oncoming traffic and the fear of putting your hand into a hot fire are healthy fears. It might be better to say that those insights are wisdom. If a person is having chest pains radiating down the arm, he should be afraid to ignore it. It is a warning that something serious may be wrong. There are people who invite trouble because they don't pay heed to healthy fear. But some kinds of fear are unhealthy and only torment us and prevent us from making progress.

The list of crippling fears that steal our quality of life is endless. How can we experience freedom from tormenting fear? I believe the only way to overcome fear is to live boldly. Boldness enables us to confront our fear and refuse to let that emotion rule us. Actually, courage is said to be progress in the presence of fear. The feelings of fear are real and can be very strong. Fear is one of the most powerful negative emotions we encounter throughout life. The longer we permit feelings of fear to rule us, the stronger they become. A person ruled by fear is said to have a spirit of fear. In other words, she functions and makes most decisions on the basis not of faith, but of fear. Those with a spirit of fear are prone to think of the worst thing that could happen rather than the best. The list of "what-ifs" is endless, and the fear of the unknown keeps them frozen in place and unable to make healthy progress in life. We all experience fear from time to time, but that is quite different from living with a spirit of fear.

I don't believe we should put up with any fear that is not healthy. When we feel strongly that we are to take a certain action, perhaps an action that God is leading us to take, and fear tries to stop us, we must "do it afraid." I have shared this simple but powerful principle in some of my other writing, but it is impossible for me to teach on fear without it. Confrontation is usually necessary for freedom. Satan works very hard to steal the freedom Jesus has provided for us, and we must be prepared to aggressively resist him at all times.

The best response when you feel fearful is to say emphatically, "I will not fear." I cannot promise that declaration will make the feeling of fear disappear, but it does let the devil know where you stand, and it is a way of reminding yourself that you have a right to live boldly, without letting fear rule you. The feelings of fear will evaporate little by little as you confront them, but they are not likely to go away on their own. Fear is the number one tool used by Satan to keep people from being in God's will and enjoying the life He has provided.

There are thousands of different fears, but the principles of how to defeat fear are the same no matter what kind we are dealing with. Following are some of the fears that are prevalent in people's lives.

Common Fears

One of the strongest and most persistent fears that people experience is the fear that they won't have what they need. We want to feel safe in every area of life. We want to be secure in our belief that we will have what we need when we need it. We may fear that we will lack adequate finances or companionship, or that we won't have the necessary strength and ability to achieve the things we need to.

Your boss may require you to work long hours for his benefit so he can make more money without offering any benefit to you. His demands take you away from your family excessively and leave you tired and worn-out. If he is a controlling person, he is probably adept at using your fear of job loss to keep you obedient to his demands, but you need to have boundaries in your life for your own protection.

We can also be afraid that we will lack the answers we need when we must make an important decision.

No matter what the fear is, God's Word says we are not to fear because He is with us. It is just that simple: "Fear not [there is nothing to fear], for I am with you" (Isa. 41:10). He has everything we need and He loves us, so like any loving parent, He will provide for us. He has promised to never leave us or forsake us. He never sleeps, He is ever present, and He keeps watch over us with loving care.

I am sure that brings the question to mind: *If God is with me, why do bad things happen to me?* God never promises us a trouble-free life, but He does promise us His presence and the strength (mental, physical, and emotional) we require to get through our troubles. This encourages me to remember that even though Daniel had to go into the lions' den, he came out unharmed. His friends Shadrach, Meshach, and Abednego had to go into the fiery furnace. They even had to endure the furnace being turned up hotter than usual, but there appeared a fourth man in the furnace (Jesus) to be with them, and eventually they also came out unharmed. The Bible even states that they went into the furnace bound and came out loosed. It was inside the furnace that they got free from their bondage! Wow! The Bible says that when they came out, they didn't even smell like smoke. (See Dan. 3; 6.)

Perhaps we should place more value on the lessons from the furnace. I have realized that we not only grow spiritually in our trials, but we grow much more than we ever do when everything is going well. No matter what the problem is, we can be assured that "this too shall pass," and we will be stronger and know God better when it is over than before it began.

> *Perhaps we should place more value on the lessons from the furnace.*

Behold! I have given you authority and power to trample upon serpents and scorpions, and [physical and mental strength and ability] over all the power that the enemy [possesses]; and nothing shall in any way harm you.   *(Luke 10:19)*

Several years ago, a friend of mine went in for a routine checkup and learned days later that her doctor feared she might have non-Hodgkin's lymphoma, the most aggressive form of the disease. More tests were needed, and she was told that it might take two or three weeks before a confirmed diagnosis could be reached.

I asked my friend how she got through those weeks of uncertainty and if she was afraid. "Yes, I was afraid," she said. "But I also knew that whatever the outcome was, it would be no surprise to God." Then she said something else that might be of help to you, whether you're fearful about a diagnosis, a possible job loss, or just about anything else. She told me that she realized if she worried for three weeks and then learned that she had lymphoma, she would have wasted three valuable weeks of her life. And if she worried for three weeks and learned that she did not have lymphoma, she would have wasted three valuable weeks of her life. "Believe it or not," she said, "I didn't lose a minute's sleep for those twenty-one days."

When the tests finally came back, my friend learned that she did indeed have non-Hodgkin's lymphoma. She had surgery and endured many months of chemo. I'm pleased to tell you that ten years later, she's in terrific health. And she didn't waste three valuable weeks.

Let's Get a New Attitude

I think that some modern believers are far too fearful of trials and trouble. At the first sign of trouble, we begin to shrink back in fear. The believers who lived in past centuries seemed to have had a different strength than most do today. We are rather accustomed to convenience and usually don't do well with suffering of any type; it frightens us. Let's remember how David faced the giant Goliath and take joy in defeating fear rather than letting it rule us. You are much more than your feelings. You are a powerful, wise, beloved child of God, and you can do whatever you need to do in life through Christ, who is your strength (see Phil. 4:13).

There may be times in our lives when God allows us to go through serious difficulties to enable us to minister to and comfort others who are suffering. If this is what God permits in our lives, then we can be assured we are able because He promises to never allow us to go through more than we can bear.

Consider the following scripture:

Blessed be the God and Father of our Lord Jesus Christ, the Father of sympathy (pity and mercy) and the God [Who is the Source] of every comfort (consolation and encouragement), Who comforts (consoles and encourages) us in every trouble (calamity and affliction), so that we may also be able to comfort (console and encourage) those who are in any kind of trouble or distress, with the comfort (consolation and encouragement) with which we ourselves are comforted (consoled and encouraged) by God.   (2 Corinthians 1:3–4)

These verses speak of encouragement. God puts courage in us so we can navigate through life without the agonizing torment of fear. God did not deliver me from the abuse I experienced in my childhood when I asked Him to, but He did strengthen me in it, and my experience has become a source of comfort to many. He did not deliver me from it, but He has delivered me from the effects of it. I can say with Shadrach, Meshach, and Abednego that there was indeed a fourth man in my fiery furnace, and I have come out of the furnace and don't even smell like smoke.

God promises a resurrection life that lifts us out from among the dead even while we are in the body (see Phil. 3:10–11). The apostle Paul stated that he was determined to know God and the power of this resurrection life. No matter what you might be going through right now, I encourage you to make a decision that God will bring you through, and you do not have to be afraid of lack in any area of your life because God is faithful.

Anytime you begin to doubt that God will come through for you, read the following scripture:

Let your character or moral disposition be free from love of money [including greed, avarice, lust, and craving for earthly possessions] and be satisfied with your present [circumstances and with what you have]; for He [God] Himself has said, I will not in any way fail you nor give you up nor leave you without support. [I will] not, [I will] not, [I will] not in any degree leave you helpless nor forsake nor let [you] down (relax My hold on you)! [Assuredly not!]

So we take comfort and are encouraged and confidently and boldly say, The Lord is my Helper; I will not

be seized with alarm [I will not fear or dread or be terri-
fied]. What can man do to me?   (*Hebrews 13:5–6*)

God instructed Joshua to lead the Israelites into the Promised Land after Moses died. Joshua had been close to Moses
and no doubt had seen firsthand the difficulties Moses experienced. Would he be able to do what Moses had done? Could
he endure the unbelief, murmuring, and complaining of the
people? Was he strong enough? Would the people respect
his leadership? God reminded Joshua that as He was with
Moses, so He would be with him. Then God told Joshua several times that all he needed to do was keep going forward.
God never promised him that he wouldn't feel fear, but he
told him to confront his fear and move past it. The word *fear*
means "to take flight or run away from." How often do we
run from things in fear when God clearly wants us to stand
firm and "do it afraid"?

Joshua could not let the feeling of fear rule him, and neither can we. God has a good plan for your life, but Satan will
use fear to make an effort to steal that good plan. It is up to us
whether we let him suc-
ceed or not. Stop waiting
for all your feelings of
fear to go away and con-
front them boldly in the
strength of God.

> *Every evening I turn my worries over
> to God. He's going to be up all
> night anyway.*
> Mary C. Crowley

Every evening I turn my worries over to God.
He's going to be up all night anyway.
Mary C. Crowley

Are You Unplugged?

There is no power shortage in heaven. God is not ever in a recession. His grace is sufficient to meet every need. What is grace? Grace is the power of the Holy Spirit coming to us freely, enabling us to do with ease what we could never do on our own. You might find other definitions stating that grace is God's divine favor and that is certainly true, but it was important to me to learn that His grace was the power I needed to live my life in victory. Grace can be received only through faith, and that is one of the main reasons why we must resist fear. When we allow fear to rule us, we unwittingly receive what Satan has planned for our lives instead of what God has planned.

Faith is our plug into the grace of God. Think of a lamp. The lamp can give light only if it is plugged into a power source. If it is unplugged, it will not work, no matter how many times we turn the switch on and off. I was once in a hotel room trying to get a lamp to work and in frustration thought, *Can't these hotels even provide a lamp that works?!* Then someone from the maintenance department came to my room, only to discover the lamp was unplugged. I ask again, "Are you unplugged?" Have you let fear steal your faith? If you have, don't worry about it. Just decide right now that you are going to have a new attitude, one that is filled with boldness, courage, and faith.

We cannot please God without faith, so it stands to reason that we must work with the Holy Spirit at all times to resist fear and stay filled with faith.

Release Your Faith

There is no doubt that fear can be intense and not something that's easily ignored. It can produce physical manifestations of shaking, dry mouth, wild thoughts, and feelings of panic. Therefore, for me to tell you, "Just ignore it," would be a bit ridiculous. But I can assure you that your faith is greater than any fear you may experience.

Faith is given to all men, according to Romans 12:3, but that faith must be unleashed for it to do any practical good. It may sound spiritual to say, "I am full of faith," but are you using your faith? How do you unleash your faith? It is so simple that I think we often miss it. Faith is released by praying, saying, and doing whatever God asks us to do. Three simple steps:

Praying

Most of us believe that prayer is powerful, so that should always be our first line of defense. We invite God to get involved in our situations through our prayers. The Bible says that tremendous power is made available through the prayers of a righteous man. Since we have been given the righteousness of God through our faith in Christ, we can come boldly to the throne of grace, and by faith, ask for help in plenty of time to meet our need (see Heb. 4:16).

Don't merely pray for the problem to go away, or that you will get something you need or desire, but also pray that God will strengthen you during your waiting period. Pray that you will have the grace to wait with a good attitude. The Bible teaches us that when we pray, if we believe we have received and do not doubt, our prayer request will be granted (see Mark 11:22–24). It does not say we will get what we ask for immediately, but we will get it. I believe that the attitude we wait with partially determines how long we have to wait. A good attitude glorifies God and is a good witness of our faith to others.

Saying

After we have prayed, it's important that we talk as if we truly believe God is working in our favor. We don't have to deny the existence of the problem, but we should talk about it as little as possible. It is also very important to include in our conversation that we believe God is involved and we are expecting a breakthrough. Hold fast your confession of faith in God!

We can be plugged into a power source and get our wires crossed and end up blowing a fuse. When we do that, we lose power. What do I mean in practical terms? When we pray and ask specifically for something and then we keep complaining as if we had never prayed at all, we are short-circuiting our faith. One positive prayer and one negative statement can bring us back to zero power. We release power when we pray, and we negate power when we complain or make any kind of negative, faithless statement.

The good news is that when we blow a fuse, we can go to the breaker box and reset everything. We can go back to God and reset our faith and mouths in the right direction. Don't feel hopeless if you have made a few mistakes.

Doing

The third ingredient in releasing your faith is to do whatever you believe God is asking you to do. Obedience is a key to our victory and shows that we have faith in God. When God told Moses to strike the rock and water would come out so the Israelites could drink, he did not obey God. Moses was angry, and he struck the rock twice instead of once as he been told to do. God told Moses that he did not honor Him in front of the Israelites by doing exactly as he had been told. True faith does what God asks it to do. When Jesus was asked by His mother to provide more wine for the wedding they were attending, she turned to the servants and said, "Whatever He says to you, do it!" They needed a miracle for the wedding party to proceed as expected, and in order to get the miracle, they needed to do exactly as Jesus instructed (see John 2:1–11).

Sometimes He even asks us to do nothing, and in that case, nothing is what we need to do. The Bible says to be still and know that He is God (see Psalm 46:10). That is often harder for me than staying active doing something. Obedience is one way of releasing our faith.

If we are hearers of the Word and not doers, we are deceiving ourselves through reasoning that is contrary to the truth (see James 1:22). Obedient action is a requirement for miracles. Jesus met a blind man who requested healing. He spat on the ground, made mud and rubbed it on the man's eyes, then told him to go wash in a pool of water. The man could have made an excuse and said, "Jesus, I am blind. How can I even find the water? And furthermore, this method of spitting and rubbing mud on my eyes seems a bit unorthodox." Jesus was predictably unpredictable. He did things differently when working with different people. I think this may have been to show that the method is not the important thing. What is important is for us to trust and do what He says.

There is no doubt that fear will come, but if you keep moving forward, it has no way to control you. Even though fear may be talking to you, that does not mean you have to listen. Satan will use fear to steal our destiny if we allow him to, but our faith has more power than fear when it is released.

Look at the Whole Picture

When we focus on what has gone wrong, it can start to seem that nothing ever goes right, but that is simply not true. I've had lots of terrible things take place in my life: abuse throughout my childhood, failure of my first marriage, breast cancer, hysterectomy, migraine headaches for ten years, loss of friends and family when called into ministry...I could go on and make the list even longer, but my point is that even with all of that, my good times have outnumbered my bad.

Look at your life as a whole rather than focusing on tragedies, trials, and disappointments. Looking at the good will give you courage to deal with the bad things and avoid living in fear. In each of the situations I mentioned above, I felt afraid, but I made it through them all with God's help. Realizing that gives me courage to face the future boldly, knowing that I truly can do all things through Christ, who strengthens me.

Fear of Inadequacy

Many of our fears are rooted in insecurity and self-doubt. What do you think of yourself? I encourage you to work with the Holy Spirit to see yourself the way God sees you. There is no power without confidence. Are you afraid that God is not pleased with you? Do you regularly inventory all your faults, past failures, and weaknesses, and then feel weak due to fear? If you do, then you are focusing on the wrong thing.

God gives us His power (grace) to enable us to do what is needed in spite of our weaknesses. In fact, the Bible says that His power is made perfect and displays itself best through our weaknesses. God purposely chooses the weak and foolish things of the world to work through so that we will give Him the glory for what is being done. God wants to amaze the world, and one of the ways He does that is by accomplishing great things through people who are weak and don't have the natural ability to complete the task at hand (see 1 Cor. 1:25–29).

When God called Moses to lead the Israelites out of Egypt and into the Promised Land, Moses gave one excuse after another as to why he could not obey. All his excuses were rooted in fear. Only faith pleases God. At one point God got so angry with Moses that He actually threatened to kill him unless he obeyed. Moses finally did take a step of faith, which manifested in obedience, and he was used mightily by God.

Jeremiah was a young man called of God to do mighty things, but he too cowered in fear. God eventually told Jeremiah that if he let the fear of man rule him, God would allow him to be overcome and defeated in front of them (see Jer. 1:17).

I experienced a lot of fear about myself, so if you are in that place right now, I can assure you that I know how you "feel." But, I am encouraging you to remember that your feelings don't convey truth; only God's Word does. You may feel that you are not what you are supposed to be, that you are strange or unusual, but the truth is we are all uniquely created by God for a special purpose and should learn how to enjoy ourselves rather than being tormented by all kinds of fears of inadequacy.

I wasted some years trying to be like other people I knew, but I found that God won't help us be anyone other than ourselves. Relax, learn to love yourself, and don't be afraid that you won't be able to do what you need to do. The truth is that none of us can do what we need to do without God's help. If we look at only what we think we can do, we will all be frightened; but if we look at Jesus and focus on Him, He will give us the courage to go forward even in the presence of fear.

Start today managing the emotion of fear, and you will progress toward the best God has for you.

Decision and confession: *I will be courageous and not let the emotion of fear rule me.*

CHAPTER
14

Handling Loss

It seems to me that the only thing we're happy to lose is weight, and even that's a painful process! Apart from that, loss is usually devastating. But like it or not, loss is an inescapable part of life, and we all experience it. It is during these times that we experience some of the most intense emotions. The word *loss* itself is often associated with major life events: the loss of a job, a marriage, a loved one. But loss isn't confined to huge crises. We go through many losses, big and small, in the course of a normal life. Our children grow up and don't need us the way they once did. We grow older and can no longer keep up the pace that we used to have.

The Holmes and Rahe Stress Scale, which measures the impact of major life events on one's health, includes forty-one events that trigger significant stress. Every event is assigned a number of points, and when the sum of those points hits 150 or more, the risk of illness goes up dramatically. It's interesting to note that eight of the top ten events are losses; the only two exceptions are marriage and marital reconciliation.

Even retirement, which is usually a wonderful time of life, involves the loss of a decades-long routine, a steady paycheck, and sometimes a sense of purpose.

Life Event	Stress Points
1. Death of a spouse	100
2. Divorce	73
3. Marital separation	65
4. Imprisonment	63
5. Death of a close family member	63
6. Personal injury or illness	53
7. Marriage	50
8. Dismissal from work	47
9. Marital reconciliation	45
10. Retirement	45

What sets loss apart from other situations is that many losses are permanent, and while a loss may someday be followed by something else that is good, the loss itself cannot be undone. When a friendship ends, you may make another friend and enjoy the same activities you enjoyed with your old friend, but the original friendship is gone forever, unless the friendship can be reconciled. You can't reminisce with your new friend about that great vacation your families took together or the time when the two of you ate at a restaurant, only to realize that neither of you had your wallet.

When a marriage ends, whether by divorce or death, that union is gone forever. While you may remarry and find great joy, perhaps even greater joy than before, the special things that made your relationship with your first husband unique are a thing of the past. While the memories will give you pleasure, they're a pale substitute for the real thing.

Once a person loses his job, even if he gets a better one later on, the sting of having been told to "go away" remains for a long time.

Go Through It, Not Around It

In *A Grace Disguised: How the Soul Grows Through Loss,* Jerry Sittser describes his experience after his wife, his mother, and his young daughter were killed in a tragic car accident. In a split second, he had lost his parent, his helpmate, and his child.

Struggling to come to terms with the tragedy he'd been plunged into, he had a dream one night. He was running west, trying to catch the setting sun and feel its warmth and its light. But he was losing the race. As he followed behind, the sun was always in front of him, heading toward the horizon. No matter how fast he ran, the sun kept its distance. In the dream, he lost hope and collapsed in the darkness.

Later on, he was describing the dream to a friend, who pointed out to him that the fastest way to reach the sun and the light of day is not to head west, chasing after the setting sun, but to head east and plunge into the darkness until the sunrise comes.

"I discovered in that moment," he said, "that I had the power to choose the direction my life would head, even if the only choice open to me, at least initially, was either to run from the loss or to face it as best I could. Since I knew that darkness was inevitable and unavoidable, I decided . . . to walk into the darkness rather than try to outrun it."

The good news is that there is something waiting for you on the other side of loss. It may be a different job, it may be a different spouse, or it may be a new ability to empathize with others who are going through a situation similar to yours. But you do have a choice. You can move through your loss and come out on the other side. The decision to move forward doesn't eliminate the emotions that we feel, but the emotions will subside as time goes by. It is important not to let our emotions control us during loss. It is best not to make rash decisions or sudden changes until we have had an opportunity to mentally adjust to the loss.

The Stages of Loss and Grief

Elisabeth Kübler-Ross was the first to recognize that there are patterns of response to loss when she studied people's experiences of death and dying in the 1970s. She learned that most people go through similar phases when they undergo a major loss, and while not everyone goes through all the stages, her findings provide a good road map of what to expect when we suffer loss. Let's discuss each of the five stages of grief:

1. Shock and Denial

Susan had been a customer service manager at a large mail-order service organization for nine years. She had worked her way up in the company from the time she was twenty-two years old, receiving good reviews and consistent promotions along the way. As manager, she had come up with a way to limit customers' waiting time on the phone to fifteen seconds or less, and she raised the efficiency of her department by 30 percent.

She was in the middle of working on a pilot program that would do away with recorded responses to customer calls entirely, and live operators were helping every inquiry.

Business was still down because of the recession, but news reports were beginning to say that the economy was turning around and things were looking up.

It was an average Thursday afternoon and the workday was winding down. When her boss called Susan into her office for their weekly meeting, Susan was ready to produce the latest figures, still improving, and possibly kick back for a few minutes and chat with her boss about their children, who were in the same grade.

The minute she walked into Renee's office, Susan could tell there'd be no chatting that day. Renee looked upset. She offered Susan a cup of coffee and then told her that the company was cutting back; that they'd done everything possible to trim their budgets, but they were still losing money. Four managers were losing their jobs, and unfortunately, Susan was one of them. She could tie up loose ends the next day and then say good-bye to her colleagues. Renee was terribly sorry; it had nothing to do with Susan's performance and everything to do with trying to keep the company afloat. Susan walked out of her boss's office in a daze. At first she couldn't believe it. Surely she was dreaming.

One minute life is good; the next, the world is turned upside down, and shock and surprise set in.

God has created us in such a way that our brains are very protective of us. The brain understands that sometimes we just can't take in the reality of a big change; it would be too overwhelming to absorb everything at once. So it refuses to let all the impact hit us right away. I like to say that God has built us with shock absorbers like a car has that soften the impact when we hit a huge pothole in the road. During this stage, you feel numb, as if you're sleepwalking. You may catch yourself just staring at the walls, unable to focus or do even everyday tasks. Out of the blue you'll shake your head and say to no one in particular, "I just can't believe it."

2. Sadness

Once the shock has begun to wear off, sadness sets in. Sometimes the pain is so intense that it emerges in physical symptoms. Fatigue, insomnia, loss of appetite, and even chest pain may occur. Waves of sadness roll over you like the ocean's tide. Just when you think you're feeling better, another one crashes up against you. Reading the Psalms can be very comforting at times like this.

3. Anger

This is the "Why me?" stage. *It just isn't fair!* Susan thought time and again. She had worked hard and done a great job for her company. Surely there was another way they could have economized without cutting her job. Why hadn't they cared enough to find a way to keep her?

Believe it or not, anger is a valuable part of the healing process. Unlike sadness, which is exhausting, anger energizes and propels us to move forward.

> When angry, do not sin; do not ever let your wrath (your exasperation, your fury or indignation) last until the sun goes down. *(Ephesians 4:26)*

I believe that anger is one of the most misunderstood emotions experienced by Christians. Many people believe it's un-Christian to get angry, but the Bible doesn't tell us not to get angry. Righteous anger is normal, unavoidable, and even healthy. But

> *Many people believe it's un-Christian to get angry, but the Bible doesn't tell us not to get angry.*

when anger bubbles and festers inside us, it creates all sorts of havoc in our minds and our bodies. It raises our blood pressure and can cause ulcers.

The Bible *does* tell us not to let the sun go down on our anger. In other words, it's best to deal with anger quickly and decisively, and don't let it control your actions.

Are you angry that your husband lost his job? That your mother is losing her health and strength? That your friend died? That's okay. Be angry. But be angry and do not sin. Don't blame God. Don't speak ill of that former boss. Scream and throw a couple of pillows around (preferably while no one else is home). Then move on, because while your anger is natural, it isn't going to change the situation. I strongly encourage talking to God openly during the entire crisis. Tell Him that you are angry and ask Him to help you handle your anger in an appropriate way.

4. Depression

After the shock, sadness, and anger have run their course, depression can set in. During depression, one's overall sense of hope for the future has been lost. Life's activities seem pointless, and a person often withdraws from connecting with friends and family. This is a normal response to loss, but if it persists for too long, it may be a good idea to see a counselor who specifically deals with the crisis experienced during major loss, or go and talk to someone who has experienced the same thing you have. A good friend of ours who is a pastor experienced the death of a son who was electrocuted under the platform in the church. To make matters worse, the accident resulted from faulty wiring that was installed by one of his church members. It took him and his wife a long time to recover from their loss, but now they help a lot of other people who have experienced the loss of a child.

Most of the time, depression born out of loss will gradually fade as the next stage comes into play. In the Psalms, David talked openly about feeling depressed, yet he refused to let the emotion control him (see Psalms 42:5–6, 11; 43:5). I would like to say again, be very careful of making major decisions during a bout of grief-induced depression. Any decisions are likely to be influenced by how you feel at the time and may not be what you will want at all when you have had time to heal.

5. Acceptance and Hope

After Susan lost her job, she went through the stages of grief over the course of several weeks. Slowly, she began to emerge from her feelings of shock and despair, and she realized that the world wasn't coming to an end. While she had taken great pride in her achievements and identity as a customer service manager, she realized that her job was only one—albeit important—facet of who she was. She was still a wife, mother, daughter, and friend. She hadn't lost her talent or her discipline or skills. She just needed to use them somewhere else. She updated her résumé and started looking for another job.

It took a few months, but Susan was able to find another position that utilized her skills…and her new company had a more generous vacation policy. By the time a couple of months had passed, Susan was happily ensconced in her new job.

I believe that when a major loss occurs, there is no place for it in our thinking. It is so shocking and painful that we simply don't know how to think about it. The greater the loss, the longer it can take to heal. Time allows us to get mentally adjusted to the way things are now, and we can finally make plans for the future.

How to Heal

You cannot prevent the birds of sorrow from
flying over your head, but you can prevent
them from building nests in your hair.
Chinese Proverb

> *You cannot prevent the birds of sorrow from flying over your head, but you can prevent them from building nests in your hair.*
> Chinese Proverb

My friend Lauren didn't get married until she was forty-five. She would often joke that by the time she met her husband-to-be, she had a better chance of sighting Elvis than of meeting the love of her life. It soon became clear, though, that Bob was indeed the love of her life; she called him "her present from God." Sometimes it was hard to believe that anyone could have such a wonderful marriage!

A little over a year ago, Bob went to the hospital for a routine gallbladder surgery. He'd been very tired and run down for several months, and Lauren was hopeful that after the surgery he'd get his old energy back and feel better than ever. A couple of days after getting home from the hospital, it was clear that something was still wrong with Bob. Lauren took him back to the hospital, where they found a "superbug" infection. While it was serious, there were antibiotics that could treat it, and Lauren was told that Bob would probably be able to come home in just a few days.

The next morning, Lauren's phone rang at 6:00 a.m. It was the hospital, calling to tell her that Bob had gone "code blue" two times during the night, and he needed emergency major surgery to save his life. He made it through the surgery, but the infection had already attacked all his major organs. For a month he remained at death's door, able to communicate with Lauren only once, when he opened his eyes and mouthed the words, "I love you." After thirty-one days in the ICU, Bob died.

Lauren was devastated. She'd waited so long to marry, and now she was a widow at the age of fifty-five, after just ten years of marriage.

I recently sat down with Lauren and asked her to tell me about her experience during the year following Bob's death. How did she cope? What did people do that was helpful? What wasn't helpful? I asked her to give my readers some of the benefit of her experience of grief. While her experience is with death, I've noticed that each point applies to many kinds of loss. Here are some of the things she shared.

1. Just Keep Breathing

Lauren told me that after Bob died, she couldn't imagine getting through the rest of her life without him. She told herself she just needed to get through the next year, which would be the hardest one, but that was too overwhelming. Little by little, she kept reducing the length of time she needed to get through in order to make it. A month was too daunting; even a week or a day felt like too much. Finally, she realized that all she had to do at any given moment was just keep breathing and eventually she would make it through. "Just keep breathing" became her motto.

I remember a time when I experienced a major loss and I kept saying, "Just get up and put one foot in front of the other." I felt I needed to just keep moving so I didn't sink into the despair I felt.

2. Don't Make Any Big Decisions or Changes for a Year

After Bob died, Lauren wanted to run away. Bob had spent two years lovingly renovating their home, and everywhere Lauren looked, she saw evidence of Bob. In fact, she had often referred to their house as Bob's love letter to her. She feared that the house would become more of a prison than a home. Lauren had also been thinking about changing jobs during the previous year. She found herself thinking about quitting her job and moving to a new city. Perhaps it was time to start over.

Early on, Lauren decided not to do anything for a year. She stayed in the house and continued working, and by the time a year had passed, she'd found that her house was a comforting place full of wonderful memories. She eventually did leave her job, but by then her thinking was clearer, and she was able to make a smooth transition to a working environment that was better for her.

3. Cry

It's okay to cry. In fact, crying is good for you. Dr. William Frey, a highly respected biochemist, led a research team that studied tears for fifteen years. They discovered that tears shed for emotional reasons are made up of different chemicals than tears that are caused by irritants or by peeling onions. The emotional tears contain toxins from the body that onion-generated tears do not contain. They concluded that chemicals that accumulate in the body during times of stress are removed from the body inside tears of sadness. Not only that, but they contain high quantities of a hormone that is one of the best indicators of stress. Suppressing those tears actually contributes to physical diseases that are aggravated by stress, including high blood pressure, heart problems, and peptic ulcers. And did you know that only humans can weep? All animals produce tears to lubricate their eyes, but only people cry because they are upset or sad.

Lauren told me that during the first few months of grieving, she would routinely get into her car and go for a "crying ride." She'd close the windows, drive down the highway, and let herself wail, scream, and cry (not to worry, she said; she could always see the road). She told me that the emotional and physical release was palpable, and that she always felt some relief by the time she pulled back into her driveway. After each big cry (on the road or at home), Lauren would tell herself that she was one good cry closer to healing, which made her feel like she was making progress.

4. Give Yourself a Break

Many of us tend to put other people's interests ahead of our own. Lauren realized that it was very important for her to cut herself more slack than usual and to pamper herself. She decided to get a massage every week and be good to herself in general. If she didn't feel like cleaning the house on a Saturday or bringing a covered dish to the church potluck supper, she didn't do it. She tried not to criticize herself for not being a superwoman. She treated herself to cut flowers and manicures. Giving herself permission to go easy on herself helped her get through those difficult first few months.

5. Mind Your Health

Researchers have learned that dealing with the death of a loved one requires the same amount of energy as working a full-time job. Which means if you're working, then you're working two full-time jobs! Other big losses are nearly as debilitating. It's easy to get into habits that are hard on your health, such as eating poorly, going to bed late, even neglecting personal hygiene like brushing your teeth. Do your best to get rest; take naps. Try to take care of your health... Getting sick will only compound your challenges.

6. Find Someone You Can Talk To

Whether you rely on friends who are there for you over the long haul or join a support group, it's vital to make sure that you don't try to "tough it out" by yourself. You'll know soon enough whom you can rely on. No matter what, it's very important to be able to talk freely with others who understand the magnitude of your loss. Lauren was fortunate to have good friends to whom she could say (almost) whatever was on her mind. She also joined a Christian support website called Grief Share (www.griefshare.org), which sends out daily e-mails filled with helpful encouragement and insights.

7. No Regrets

Even though Lauren and Bob treasured each other, she was haunted by a brief exchange that took place not long before Bob got sick. He had told her that he missed hearing her play the piano. Tired from a long day at work and still cleaning up from dinner, Lauren retorted, "And when exactly might I have time to do that?" In his usual gracious manner, Bob said nothing, and Lauren forgot about her comment until after Bob's death. But once she remembered it, she'd often think of that cutting remark and start to cry. *Why had she been so mean to the man who loved her unconditionally?* Finally, she began to realize that she's just human; that she was tired and impatient that day, and she had no idea what lay ahead so very soon. Bob wouldn't want her to beat herself up over this, and certainly not while she was in the throes of grief. He would want her to think of the love they shared and the happy memories they'd made over the years.

Regret is not a very useful emotion. You can't undo what's been done, but you can hinder your healing and make yourself sick. Learn from your past mistake and resolve not to repeat it. Then let it go.

> *Learn from your past mistake and resolve not to repeat it. Then let it go.*

8. Remind Yourself That You Won't Always Feel This Way

There are two versions of an old tale about an ancient king who called all his counselors and wise men together and gave them a challenge. One version says he asked them to summarize the wisdom of the world. The other version says the king ordered his wise men to come up with a sentence that would always be true, no matter what the situation. In both versions of the story, the sentence that met the king's requirement was "This too shall pass."

Lauren reminded herself frequently that things would change. That change might be slow, but she wouldn't always be in such terrible pain. She told me that she is making progress. She doesn't cry as much as she did, she enjoys things now that had not held her interest for a long time, and—most important—she has hope for the future.

9. Write About It

Consider keeping a journal. There's something about writing that helps us work through difficult issues. Maybe that's because your journal is one of the few places where you don't have to censor yourself or worry about a reaction to your words. It is also a chronicle of your journey that will serve you well. As you read through it, you can get an objective view of the progress you've made. Lauren hadn't realized that she was making strides until she looked back over a few months' entries and noticed that she no longer tossed and turned for hours before falling asleep. Being able to see healing progress in black and white will help you realize that you are indeed moving ahead.

10. Forgive

Well-meaning people will say things that will upset or offend you. The day after the first anniversary of Bob's death, one of Lauren's coworkers came up to her and said, "Well, it's been a year; you okay now?" *No!* Lauren wanted to say. *I'm not okay!* But she knew that her colleague was doing her best to be empathetic and encouraging. So she smiled and said,

"I'm doing better, thanks." Remember that even if they don't always say the right thing, people are trying to be supportive. You can be gracious and appreciate their intentions, even if they don't always succeed.

If someone's unjust treatment of you caused the loss you have experienced, be sure to forgive them completely. Feeling hatred and unforgiveness is like taking poison and hoping it will kill your enemy. All the bitter feelings we experience when we are treated unjustly hurt only us, and not the person who hurt us.

11. Remember That There Are Still Things to Be Thankful For

Finally, Lauren told me that one of the most healing things she did after Bob's death was to remember to be thankful for the good things she still had. Every morning on the way to work, she'd pray. In the beginning, she simply told God how she was feeling. One day it occurred to her that all she was doing was complaining, and God must be getting bored and annoyed. So she thanked Him for giving her Bob for ten years. That changed everything. She thought of more things she was thankful for: all the wonderful memories she had; the fact that of all the people in the world, God had chosen *her* to give Bob to. Then she thanked Him for her home; for the blue sky and crisp breeze and pink flowers. Before she knew it, Lauren was spending more time in prayer thanking God than complaining to Him. And she felt better too.

12. Rely on God's Comfort

> When the righteous cry for help, the Lord hears, and delivers them out of all their distress and troubles. The Lord is close to those who are of a broken heart and saves such as are crushed with sorrow.   *(Psalm 34:17–18)*

Lauren told me that she believes God mourns with us when we suffer a great loss. I think she's right. After all, when Jesus taught us to pray, He told us to call God "Abba," which is best translated as "Daddy." What daddy doesn't ache when his little boy comes home defeated after striking out at his Little League game? What mother doesn't feel her own heart break as her little girl comes home from school having been taunted on the playground? In the overall scheme of things, these are tiny losses and hurts, and the parent knows that. But the pain of seeing your child suffering is piercing nonetheless.

Immediately after teaching the disciples to pray what we know as the Lord's Prayer, Jesus asked, "What man is there of you, if his son asks him for a loaf of bread, will hand him a stone? Or if he asks for a fish, will hand him a serpent?" (Matt. 7:9–10). In other words, because He is our Father, God suffers when we suffer. And while He could change our circumstances in an instant, more often than not, He doesn't. But when He sees His child suffer, He suffers too.

When you are feeling loss and sorrow, ask God to hold you in the hollow of His hand, to whisper His comfort and to stroke your head, like a parent fussing over His fevered child.

You may or may not *feel* that comfort, but God's Word is true, and so is He.

How to Help a Friend Who Has Suffered Loss

Believe it or not, it's very easy to help a friend who has suffered a loss. We tend to want to offer a solution to our friend's suffering, but what they really need and want is understanding. Once when I was going to a funeral I told God that I simply did not know what to say to the person and He said, *They just need you to sit with them.* During painful loss, people need someone to listen to them talk about the loss and what they are feeling, and quite often it is better not to try to give advice because most of what we would say wouldn't help them anyway.

A friend of mine experienced the death of her youngest son. She asked to meet with me and of course I wanted to help her, but I noticed that most of what I offered as advice made her angry or defensive. At first I was hurt, but then I realized that her pain was too intense to allow her to hear advice; she needed someone to listen and simply keep telling her that she would make it through the tragedy.

Below are a few good things to say—and a few things *not* to say. But the most important thing to remember is this: What you say isn't really important. What *is* important is just to be there for your friend. When in doubt, just say, "How are you doing?" She'll take it from there.

Good Things to Say

- "I can't imagine how you feel, but I want you to know I'm very sorry that you're going through so much."
- "Anytime you want to talk, I want to be there for you. I may not know what to say, but I'll listen with love."
- "How are you doing?"
- "I wish you didn't have to go through this."
- "I want you to know that I'm praying for you."

What Not to Say

- "I know how you feel."
- "It's time to get on with your life."
- "You're so strong...you can handle it."

What to Do

1. Send a Card

A sympathy card is a gift. It's an even better gift if you add a handwritten line or two. It doesn't have to be long. Just a heartfelt sentence saying something like the following will be like salve on a wound: "I know this is a terribly difficult time for you, and I want you to know that you're especially in my thoughts and prayers right now."

If you knew the person who died, a brief reminiscence is tremendously comforting. For example: "I remember Tom's beautiful smile...He had a way of making me feel so special whenever we spoke."

If your friend has lost a job or her health, a card is a wonderful way to show her that you care.

2. Pick up the Phone—Especially Later

Within a few weeks of a funeral, the initial wave of sympathy to the bereaved passes. Then the days become long and lonely. Most people go back to their lives and the grieving person is left by themselves. Suddenly the mailbox is full of the usual bills and catalogs and the telephone is silent. A brief phone call to just say, "I've been thinking of you. How are you?" will be a gift to your friend that she'll never forget. Do it every now and then; any time is a good time.

3. Touch Your Friend

When you see the person who suffered the loss, you can give comfort through physical touch. Take her hand and squeeze it gently; give her a warm hug or a simple pat on the back. Loving touch is one of the ways we show love.

Decision and confession: *With God's help I will recover from my loss and be thankful for what I still have.*

CHAPTER
15

*Freedom from Discouragement
and Depression*

What is depression? *Webster's Dictionary* says it is "the act of pressing down; a low state. A hollow place, a sinking of the spirits; dejection; a state of sadness; lack of courage or strength."

People who are depressed lose interest in things they previously enjoyed, and they often experience changes in sleep or eating habits. They may feel worthless or be unable to concentrate. They may feel lonely and hopeless. I think the feeling of depression is one of the worst feelings there is. I can honestly say that if I had a choice between the emotional pain of depression or some type of physical pain, I would prefer physical pain.

The Bible does not use the term "depression," but instead refers to the feeling as being "downcast." Depression is a feeling, and this book is geared toward teaching how to control our feelings rather than allowing them to control us. Can we control depression? I believe the answer is yes. I don't think anyone has to permanently live with depression. All of us experience a low-mood day now and then. Sometimes it is because of a disappointment or a loss, but at other times we really don't know why we feel the way we do. If it's just a day here and there, I don't think there is much to be concerned about. We are complex beings with many intricate parts that all have to work well together for optimum health. Some days we just don't feel well physically or emotionally, and it is usually best to not worry about it, get some rest, and we will probably feel better the next day.

In this chapter I would like to look at two kinds of depression. The first type, "medical depression," is caused by something physical that we cannot control. The second type is "situational depression." That is depression caused by our response to circumstances in life. There is help available for both, but the treatment is different for each type.

Medical Depression

I am not a doctor, but I do know it's common knowledge that hormone imbalances, neurotransmitter imbalances, and thyroid disorders are at the top of the list of root causes of depression that has a medical source. Various brain disorders or cardiac conditions can also cause depression. At one point I began to notice that I was feeling sad and down each morning for about two hours, and then I seemed to get over it for the remainder of the day. I thought I was just tired or thinking negatively and needed to "cheer up," but when I went to the doctor for my regular checkup, he noticed that my thyroid was borderline low. He said that because the levels were in the acceptable range, it would normally not be treated, but because I had told him I was experiencing low moods, he put me on a very low dose of natural thyroid. I can honestly say that when I took the first pill, the mild feeling of depression I had experienced disappeared and has not returned.

Because of the stress that most people live under today, many have neurotransmitter imbalances that may cause low serotonin levels in the blood. Serotonin is referred to as the happy hormone, and if we don't have enough of it, we are likely to simply not feel happy. Serotonin levels can be altered through medicine, but it is wise to try to correct them naturally if we can. Eliminating excessive stress, as well as eating a proper diet and exercising, can help immensely to balance the brain chemicals.

Many women experience depression after giving birth or during their monthly cycle simply because of hormonal changes in their bodies. These changes may be temporary or they might require some medical attention. The point I want to make is that not all depression can be cured without medical attention, and I don't want anyone to feel condemned if they have to take medicine for depression. On the other hand, I believe that some doctors, including psychiatrists, often hand out pills too quickly without even searching for other medical conditions that may be causing the depression. I also want to encourage people who do have to take medicine to realize they may not always have to take it.

I know a woman who was going through a very stressful time in her life and began to have panic attacks. She went to her doctor, who encouraged her to take a medicine for anxiety, and it did help her almost immediately. She not only took medicine but she made some lifestyle changes to help reduce stress and made a decision not to worry about things she had no control over. After about six months the woman wanted to see if she could get off the medicine. She slowly cut it down until she was able to get off it completely and has been fine ever since.

Even if depression is caused by medical reasons, the things I am going to share about situational depression will help people confront the feelings of a low mood for any reason. Recovering from depression usually requires a well-rounded treatment program that includes things like learning to think differently, laughing more, and worrying less. As I said, I am not a doctor, but I have been teaching the Bible for more than thirty years, and I am certain that we do not have to let our situations and circumstances in life depress us.

Situational Depression

Most people who experience trouble, disappointment, or tragedy are tempted to sink into depression. Because our moods are directly linked to our thoughts and words, when our thoughts descend into negative territory, our moods tend to follow. We can easily depress ourselves merely by thinking and talking about everything that is wrong in our lives and the world in general. When God gave us the ability to control our thoughts, He gave us a wonderful ability. We have the ability to cheer ourselves up no matter what our circumstances are. Sadly, a lot of people

> When God gave us the ability to control our thoughts, He gave us a wonderful ability. We have the ability to cheer ourselves up no matter what our circumstances are.

don't know this wonderful truth. It is easy to go through life with a victim mentality, simply believing that you can do nothing about the way you feel, especially if you have encountered a major disappointment in life.

Here is one simple solution the Bible gives for depression: Put on the garment of praise for the spirit of heaviness (see Isa. 61:3). What God offers us is greater than anything the enemy offers. Praise will neutralize sadness, but we must remember that we are instructed to "put on" praise. We cannot be passive and merely hope the sad feeling goes away.

I have been reading a Christian classic by Hannah Whitehall Smith titled *The Christian's Secret to a Happy Life*. I was amazed and encouraged when I read that, despite the difficulties she encountered in her life, she made a decision that she would always believe God—with or without feelings, in good times and in bad.

Hannah married Robert Smith when she was nineteen years old. He seemed to be a very devout and romantic young man who managed a family-owned business. However, it soon became clear that he was impulsive and emotional. He was also inclined to make rash and unwise decisions, in both his business and his personal life. Robert bankrupted the business. After having had a strong encounter with God, Robert began to preach the Gospel. His preaching ministry was abruptly ended by accusations of sexual misconduct. His health deteriorated and he eventually had a nervous breakdown. Through all these difficulties, Hannah continued to trust God and frequently said, as did Job, "Even though He slay me, yet will I trust Him."

Hannah and Robert had seven children, but four of them died. One daughter was stillborn. Her oldest son, Frank, died at the age of eighteen from typhoid fever. Her daughter Nellie died at the age of five from bronchitis. On Hannah's birthday, February 7, her eleven-year-old Rachel died of scarlet fever. But Hannah clung to her faith tenaciously through all these difficulties.

She became a trusted and sought-after Bible teacher and preacher. She experienced a real crisis in her faith when she diligently sought evidence of the Baptism of the Holy Spirit or, as it was often called in those days, the second blessing. Many people she knew, including Robert, had glorious experiences, but she never did. Filled with self-doubt about her faith until it almost drove her to despair, she made the decision to receive the fullness of the Holy Spirit by faith alone and to never doubt God again. Hannah learned in her life that her own effort to achieve holiness was useless and that she must depend wholly on God to do the work in her. This complete dependence became the bedrock of her faith.

Robert died in unbelief and her adult children lost their faith. In 1911 she died peacefully at the age of seventy-nine. Throughout her life she never lost her faith or dishonored God. Hannah was able to say, "I have given my best and could do no more." Although writing was a labor of love for her and not something she really enjoyed, *The Christian's Secret of a Happy Life* has been in print for 125 years and has sold millions of copies.

I hesitated to tell Hannah's story because I don't want to leave the impression that the Christian life is one that is filled with only tragedy and sorrow because it isn't that way at all. But I do want to strongly make the point that even though her circumstances were tragic, God led her through it all, used her mightily, and she apparently was quite happy during most of her life—happy enough to write a book on happiness! Hannah's joy was in Jesus, not her circumstances.

Most of us won't experience the degree of difficulties that Hannah did, although some may, and the reasons why must be left in the hands of God.

Have a Chat with Yourself

When I realize I am in a bad mood, I often have a chat with myself. I say, "Joyce, what's your problem? Look at how blessed you are, Joyce, and stop feeling sorry for yourself. Get your mind on something that will cheer you up and try doing something nice for someone else." It is amazing what good results I get just from reasoning with myself; you should try it!

The psalmist David asked himself a question when he was feeling downcast. He said, "Why are you cast down, O my inner self? And why should you moan over me and be disquieted within me? Hope in God and wait expectantly for Him, for I shall yet praise Him, my Help and my God" (Psalm 42:5; also see 42:11; 43:5). David's solution for depression was to hope in God and expect something good to happen. He told himself to put on praise while he was waiting for a change in his circumstances.

This is certainly a great example of someone not letting

his feelings manage him. David made a decision that had nothing to do with how he felt.

There are other places in Scripture where David describes feeling very low and discouraged, and with good reason. He had many enemies, and God did not always deliver him from them quickly. David was anointed to be king of Israel twenty years before he actually wore the crown. Because of his jealousy and fear, the king in power at the time, Saul, tried multiple times to kill him. David literally hid in caves for many years, waiting for God to do something. No wonder he had to chat with himself often and make a decision not to let his emotions control him. He looked beyond how he felt to the God he knew to be faithful.

You can fight the feelings of depression by reminding yourself of blessings in your life. You can listen to music or sing. Even getting your mind off yourself by doing something kind for someone else will help immensely. Don't forget that our moods are connected to our thoughts; therefore, I urge you to take notice of what you're thinking about when you feel depressed. You may find the source of your problem.

Talking about past victories in your life can also be a way to cheer yourself up. Fight the good fight of faith and do everything you can to help yourself. Compared to eternity, our days on earth are short, and we want to enjoy each one of them. Depression and joy simply can't dwell in the same heart, so I urge you to find so many things to be happy about that there is no room left for depression.

The Root of Depression

Situational depression always has a root source. Quite often it is disappointment. When expectations are defeated or desire is frustrated, we usually feel disappointed, and it is understandable to feel that way. If I put a lot of effort into a thing and it bears no fruit, then I feel that I wasted my time and start to feel discouraged. I am sure a farmer would feel that way if he did all he could to ensure a good crop and right before harvest time a storm came and destroyed it.

Dashed expectations lead to disappointment. We expect certain things and behaviors from people and yet we don't always get what we expect. Sometimes the way people behave shocks us and leaves us disappointed. We also expect certain things from ourselves and then let ourselves down. We expect things from God, and for reasons known only to Him, He doesn't do what we expect. The best thing to do when we feel disappointed is to get reappointed. Shake off the disappointment and get a new dream, vision, goal, or plan. Often, the best medicine for a woman who has had a miscarriage is to get pregnant again as soon as it is safe for her health. The same principle will work for you anytime you get disappointed. In God, there is always a place of new beginnings. It is never too late to begin again! Each morning when the sun rises it declares, "It is a new day; let's start over."

Discouragement is another root of depression. The discouraged person is disheartened; she feels like quitting or giving up; she has lost hope and feels no courage to keep going. When we are deeply discouraged, everything about us feels down. Discouragement can come from being disappointed, or you might feel that you're in a season when life seems hard to deal with, or there seems to be trouble everywhere you turn.

I mentioned earlier that I am having some back problems right now, and one of the things that irritates the pain is excessive sitting. I can't write standing up, so I could get discouraged. I need to meet a deadline, so I need to do the writing now. Instead of getting into a spirit of discouragement, I am adapting and getting up frequently to stretch, using ice to combat the inflammation and taking plenty of acetaminophen. Naturally I've thought, *Why does this have to happen now, of all times?* I didn't get an answer, which is normally the case when we ask, "Why, God, why?"

Several people have remarked that I have a good attitude about this situation. It would not be cool if I were writing a book about not letting our emotions control us at the same time I was letting mine control me! I think it is important for you to realize that everyone has challenges, including me, and they are never convenient.

Discouragement

Sometimes we see the prosperity of the wicked and that discourages us. As children of God, we expect to be blessed more than those who are not serving God. We might paraphrase a portion of Psalm 73 this way: "It looked to me as if the wicked were better off than the righteous, until I realized God's patience does run out and He will deal with them."

It is a serious mistake to look at what other people have and compare it to what you have. God has an individual and unique plan for each of us, and comparison only tends to be a source of discouragement or pride. If we feel we are better off than others, we may become prideful (thinking more highly of ourselves than we should); if we feel they are better off than us, we may become discouraged and even depressed.

The Bible emphatically states that the wicked in the end will be cut off, but the righteous shall inherit the land. I don't think "the end" necessarily means the end of the world or the end of our lives. I think it means when all is said and done, in due time (God's time), the blessings of the child of God will surpass those of the wicked. The Word of God says in Galatians 6:9 that if we refuse to become weary in well doing, in due time we shall reap if we don't faint.

Another root source of depression and discouragement is feeling bad about yourself. Feeling ashamed of who you are or suffering from abnormal guilt can easily make you depressed. If you don't like yourself, the bad feelings you have inside will be a continual source of inner pain. It is vital that you learn to accept and respect the person God made you to be. All of our behavior may be far from what it needs to be, but if we are willing to change, God will keep working with us, and every day we will get better and better in every way. Don't despise yourself because of your imperfections; instead, learn to celebrate your successes, even small ones.

If you are depressed, try to determine what the root source is. Is it medical? Have you been deeply disappointed? Are you discouraged? Have you experienced a loss in your life? Do you compare yourself with others? Do you feel a lot of shame or guilt because of past mistakes or being hurt by other people? Do you get enough rest? Do you maintain balance in your life? What are your eating habits? Are you deep in debt? Do you have good friends whom you enjoy? Understanding the source of depression may help you overcome it.

Despair

Have you ever felt true despair? It is a place of total hopelessness. The person in despair feels that there is no way out of his or her situation. The psalmist David said that he would have despaired had he not believed that he would see the goodness of God in the land of the living. He knew that if he allowed himself to become totally hopeless, despair would ensue. He avoided getting to that place by continuing to believe that something good was going to happen (see Psalm 27:13). In his classic *My Utmost for His Highest*, Oswald Chambers pointed out that when Jesus said, "Let not your heart be troubled," He was affirming that we do have control over how we will react to our circumstances. "God will not keep your heart from being troubled," Chambers said. "It is a command—'Let not...' Haul yourself up a hundred and one times a day in order to do it, until you get into the habit of putting God first and calculating with Him in view."

Even if you have a difficult time saying that you truly believe something good will happen, start by saying it out loud again and again, and soon you will start believing it.

Suicides are increasing rapidly. One national hotline that takes calls 24-7 reported that in April 2007, 38,114 people called the hotline. In April 2009 the same hotline received 51,465 calls. That is an alarming increase that I believe has a lot to do with world conditions and negative media.

Four out of every 10 callers reported financial stress as one of their problems. A downturn in the economy can affect our attitudes and create fear and depression if we do not keep our hope in God rather than in the world system.

A *Charlotte Observer* story provides some startling statistics about suicide attempts in North Carolina. Charlotte police reported a 55 percent increase in suicide attempts over the previous year. A county suicide hotline fielded three thousand more calls in March 2009 than in March 2008, and a local hospital saw a 9 percent increase in patients who'd attempted or considered suicide. Dr. Paula Clayton, medical director for the American Foundation for Suicide Prevention, stated that for every suicide, there are probably one hundred attempts.

Most of us have at some time or another in life felt that we just could not go on and momentarily wished we were dead or thought of putting an end to it all. Even the great prophet Elijah told God that if he was going to constantly have enemies after him, he would rather be dead. It is one thing to have a momentary, fleeting thought of suicide; it is quite another to either attempt or be successful at committing it. How tragic when someone is in such despair that they would rather be dead than go on living. Jesus died so we could have and enjoy a wonderful, powerful, prosperous life, but we must resist every attempt the devil makes to steal it from us.

Habits and Decisions

Depression and discouragement can become responsive habits for some people. It is the way they respond to disappointment or trials of any kind. I had a habit of feeling sorry for myself when I didn't get my way, but I broke that habit with God's help and have formed the better habit of choosing to be happy whether I get my way or not. I try to trust God to help me acquire what He wants me to have, not merely what I want to have. It may sound overly simplified for me to say, "Break the habit of depression." But for some people, it could be just that simple. You may have had a parent who was depressed and you grew up thinking it was just the way to be, so your habit became the same as theirs. My father was very negative and I became just like him, until I learned that I could choose to be positive.

I strongly encourage you to begin managing depression or any other related moods. Life is too precious a gift to waste any of it living in the black, empty hole of depression.

Decision and confession: *Depression and discouragement will not control me. I will be happy and enjoy my life.*

CHAPTER
16

Why Is It So Hard to Forgive?

From Genesis to Revelation, we read of God's forgiveness toward us and of our need to forgive others. It is one of the main themes of the Bible. We're very eager to receive forgiveness, but we often find it extremely difficult to offer others the forgiveness that we have freely received from God. We may want to forgive, try to forgive, and pray to be able to forgive, and yet we remain bitter, resentful, and filled with angry and unforgiving thoughts. Why? If we want to forgive, why is it so difficult to do so?

The culprit is emotions. Fortunately, you can learn how to manage your emotions rather than allowing them to manage you. Forgiving those who have hurt us is one of the main areas where we need to apply what we are learning.

What can you expect from your emotions once you begin to operate in forgiveness toward yourself or others? God is ready and willing to forgive you, but are you equally ready and willing to receive His forgiveness? Your emotions can get in the way. You may not "feel" worthy of receiving such a wonderful and undeserved gift from God. You may "feel" that somehow you need to pay for what you have done wrong. You "feel" that you must sacrifice in some way in order to pay for your sins. If you do feel that way, I totally understand and can even say it is quite normal, but I also must say it is not God's will for you. I persecuted myself for many years trying to pay a debt that Jesus had already paid. I sacrificed my joy by refusing to let myself enjoy anything because of my feelings of guilt. Thankfully, I have finally realized through God's Word that I cannot pay a debt that has already been paid, and the only thing I can do with a free gift is receive it or reject it. God's gift of forgiveness is free, and we should receive it as an act of faith.

We are to freely forgive others just as we have been freely forgiven. Forgiveness is a gift and cannot truly be deserved. How can anyone undo what has hurt or wounded you? My father stole my innocence through sexual abuse. How could he ever pay me back or undo what he did? The only way for me to be free was to forgive him and trust God for restoration. Although it was one of the most difficult things in my life to do, it was helpful for me to remember that God continually forgives me and never holds any of my sins against me.

Be gentle and forbearing with one another and, if one has a difference (a grievance or complaint) against another, readily pardoning each other; even as the Lord has [freely] forgiven you, so must you also [forgive]. *(Colossians 3:13)*

What's the hardest thing you've ever been challenged to forgive? Has a friend betrayed you? Have you been so hurt by your spouse that your marriage couldn't survive and ended in a divorce? Has your child been ungrateful and unloving?

I want to tell you about a woman whose hurt can hardly be measured. In January 1990, Sue Norton received the terrible news that her mother and father had been found murdered in their Oklahoma home. The killer walked away with an old truck and $17,000 in cash.

While she sat through the murder trial of Robert B. K. Knighton, she could feel the hatred in the air as her parents' family and friends crowded the courtroom. By the last day of the trial, Norton knew that hatred wasn't going to heal her of the terrible loss she had sustained. That evening she couldn't sleep, and she spent the night praying for God to help her. The next morning, she had this thought: *Sue, you don't have to hate B.K. You could forgive him.*

Forgive him?

That morning, as the jury deliberated, Sue got permission to visit B.K. in the holding cell. She recalls that when she saw him, she didn't think of him as a killer. She thought of him as a human being. She said to the big man with steely eyes, "I don't know what to say to you, but I want you to know that I don't hate you. My grandmother...taught me that we are here to love one another. If you are guilty, I forgive you."

At first, the man thought she was playing some sort of mind game with him. He couldn't fathom that someone could forgive him for such a heinous crime. Today Robert Knighton resides on death row in Oklahoma. Sue writes him frequently, and she occasionally visits him. Because of her love and friendship, he has become a devout Christian.

Friends think she has lost her mind. But Sue says, "There is no way to heal and get over the trauma without forgiveness. You must forgive and get on with your life. That is what Jesus would do."

Scripture makes it very clear that God expects us to forgive readily and freely. But our emotions flare up and aggressively resist our making this decision. Is there anything that can help us get past the emotions and obey God in this area?

Three Things That Help Me Forgive

The first thing that really helps me forgive is to remember that *God forgives me for much more than I will ever have to forgive others for.* We may

> *God forgives me for much more than I will ever have to forgive others for.*

not do what others have done to us, but then again we may do things that are worse. In God's kingdom sin does not come in sizes like small, medium, and large; sin is just sin! Some sins leave more devastation than others, but God forgives them all. Some things that people do hurt us worse than other things, but the answer is the same for dealing with them all. Do yourself a favor and forgive quickly and freely. The longer you hold a grudge, the more difficult it is to let it go.

The second thing that helps me forgive is to think of God's mercy. Mercy is the most beautiful gift we can give or receive. It cannot be earned and is not deserved—otherwise, it wouldn't be mercy. I like to think of mercy as looking beyond *what* was done wrong and on to *why* it was done. Many times people do a hurtful thing and don't even know why they are doing it, or they may not realize they are doing it. Sometimes they are reacting to their own pain without realizing they are hurting others. I was hurt so badly in my childhood that I in turn frequently hurt others with my harsh words and attitudes. But I did not even realize I was being harsh; because life had been so hard and painful for me, that harshness had become part of me. It was just simply the way I was. It was easy for God to show me mercy because He saw why I was doing what I was doing. He saw the hurt little girl who had become hardened as a method of protecting herself from more pain.

It helps me forgive when I realize that "hurting people hurt people." When I am trying to navigate through my pain, I often have to talk to myself. I remind myself to believe the best of every person. I think, *I doubt that the person who hurt me did it on purpose.* Then I remind myself that there is a reason why they did what they did. Perhaps no one will ever know what that reason was except God, but there is always a reason. Sometimes the reason is simply that the person who hurt us does not know God, or does not know how to call on His power to help them resist temptation. Actually thinking through these various scenarios helps my emotions to calm down and makes it easier to forgive.

The third thing that helps me forgive others is to remember that if I stay angry, I am giving Satan a foothold in my life (see Eph. 4:26–27). When I forgive I am keeping Satan from gaining an

> *If I stay angry, I am giving Satan a foothold in my life.*

advantage over me (see 2 Cor. 2:10–11). Actually, one of the most valuable things I have learned is that I am doing myself a favor when I forgive. If I don't forgive, I am poisoning my own soul with bitterness that will surely work its way out in some kind of bad behavior or attitude.

The root of bitterness contaminates and defiles not only the one who is bitter, but others around him as well.

Exercise foresight and be on the watch to look [after one another], to see that no one falls back from and fails to secure God's grace (His unmerited favor and spiritual blessing), in order that no root of resentment (rancor, bitterness, or hatred) shoots forth and causes trouble and bitter torment, and the many become contaminated and defiled by it.   (Hebrews 12:15)

Bitterness and Bondage

When the children of Israel were about to be led out of Egypt, they were told by the Lord on the eve of their departure to prepare a Passover meal that included bitter herbs. Why? God wanted them to eat those bitter herbs as a reminder of the bitterness they had experienced in bondage. Bitterness belongs to bondage! If we want to avoid bondage, we must avoid bitterness.

The word *bitterness* is used to refer to something that is pungent or sharp to the taste. It is said that the bitter herbs the Israelites ate were probably akin to horseradish. If you have ever taken a big bite of horseradish, you know it can cause quite a physical reaction. Bitterness causes precisely the same type of reaction in us spiritually. Not only does it cause us discomfort, but it also causes discomfort to the Holy Spirit, who abides within us.

The Bible teaches us not to grieve (vex or sadden) the Holy Spirit by letting bitterness, indignation, and wrath abide in us. We are to banish it from ourselves! (See Eph. 4:30–31.)

How does bitterness get started? According to the Bible, it grows from a root. The King James Version speaks of a "root of bitterness" (see Heb. 12:15). Roots always produce fruit, and in this case the fruit is poisonous.

What is the seed from which that root sprouts? Unforgiveness! Bitterness results from the many minor offenses committed against us that we just won't let go of, the things we rehearse again and again inside until they become blown out of proportion and grow to a troublemaking size. I recall occasions when Dave and I argued in the early years of our marriage, and instead of dealing with the issue at hand, I brought up many other issues. Some were things that had happened years before. Dave asked me where I kept all that information stored! He is such a positive and forgiving person that he couldn't imagine my retaining every offense he had ever committed against me. Until I learned a better and wiser way to live, I let all those little things pile up inside me, just waiting for the moment when I could haul them out and use them as ammunition. I had been given a wonderful, godly man but did not know how to appreciate the gift God had given me because I stored up little offenses and refused to let them go.

Aside from all the minor things we might allow to be blown out of proportion, there are sometimes major offenses committed against us. The longer we allow our bitterness and resentment to grow and fester, the more of a problem they become and the harder it is to be free from them. Hopefully, it is obvious by now that the best thing to do regarding any offense, large or small, is to forgive quickly and completely.

> To be wronged is nothing unless you
> continue to remember it.
> *Confucius*

What We Don't Feed Becomes Weak and Dies

I mentioned earlier that the more we feed a negative emotion, the stronger it becomes; the less we feed it, the weaker it becomes. We can feed feelings of unforgiveness by simply meditating on and talking about what the person has done who hurt us. If you want to forgive someone, you must make a commitment to stop focusing on what was done to you. One way we feed bitterness is by telling others so they will feel sorry for us, but it is a dangerous thing to do, especially if we keep doing it again and again. At times it is healthy to express how you feel about something that has been painful. As I said earlier in the book, secrets can make us sick. I am not suggesting that we need to live lonely lives, never sharing our pain with anyone, but harping on something continually is quite different from sharing in a healthy way.

I have learned that once I make a decision to forgive—to let the offense go and forget it—I must also stop talking about it unnecessarily. The more I pay attention to the offense, the

> *Once I make a decision to forgive—to let the offense go and forget it—I must also stop talking about it unnecessarily.*

more strength I give it. But if I ignore it, then it is easier to get over it emotionally.

We all want justice when we have been hurt, and it's often difficult to be patient while God brings it. We are very tempted to take revenge instead of remembering that God said vengeance is His, not ours.

We know Him Who said, Vengeance is Mine [retribution and the meting out of full justice rest with Me]; I will repay [I will exact the compensation], says the Lord. And again, The Lord will judge and determine and solve and settle the cause and the cases of His people.   (Hebrews 10:30)

The Worst-Laid Plans

There have been times when I've found myself planning what I will do to get back at someone who has hurt me. I have also been guilty of thinking about the good things I've done in the past for that person that I won't do anymore. I will either hurt the person or withhold blessings, and neither one of these plans exhibits the character of Jesus. One night I lay in bed after hearing that a certain person who was a business associate was saying unkind and critical things about me, and the more I thought about what I would say to them, the more upset I became. My emotions were so stirred up that I couldn't sleep. As I continued my unkind, unloving, ungodly thoughts, I felt a nudge from the Holy Spirit. He let me know that He had a better plan. He suggested that I forget the unkind remarks that had been made about me and instead send the person who spoke them a gift and let them know how much I appreciated them. The thought of it made me laugh, and right away I saw that God's ways give us joy, while our ways often make us miserable.

As soon as I switched my thinking over to God's plan, I no longer felt the rage I had felt previously. I was still hurt and my emotions were wounded, but thinking of doing things God's way enabled me to make a decision based on His Word rather than on my feelings. I lay in bed thinking of what gift I would give the person and what I would say in the accompanying note. As soon as the office opened the next morning, I asked my assistant to order the gift. And guess what: I felt instant relief from the agony I had experienced the previous evening! When I saw the person afterward, I still felt a twinge of pain, but it was minor compared to what it could have been.

The person who spoke unkindly about me never knew that I was aware, but God knew, and He is the One who recompenses us for the injustices in our lives.

Emotions Follow Decisions

Our responsibility is to make right decisions based on God's Word, and His job is to heal our emotions. We usually want to feel better first, but God wants us to do what is right first, no matter how we feel. When we do, we are growing spiritually and will enjoy more emotional stability

> *Our responsibility is to make right decisions based on God's Word, and His job is to heal our emotions. We usually want to feel better first, but God wants us to do what is right first, no matter how we feel.*

the next time we are faced with a difficult situation. When we make a decision to forgive, we probably won't feel like forgiving. After all, we have been treated unjustly, and it hurts. But doing the right thing while we feel wronged is extremely important to our overall spiritual growth. It also glorifies God.

For many years I tried to forgive people when they hurt or offended me, but since I still had negative feelings toward them, I assumed that I wasn't successful in the forgiveness journey. Now I realize that no matter how I feel, if I keep praying for the person who injured me and bless rather than curse him or her, I am on my way to freedom from destructive emotion. To curse means to speak evil of, and to bless means to speak well of. When someone has hurt us, we can refuse to speak evil of them, even if we're tempted to do so. We can also bless them by talking about their good qualities and good things they have done. If we only look at the mistakes people make, we won't be able to like them. But looking at their whole lives gives us a more balanced picture of them.

Nothing I have said will keep you from experiencing emotional pain when someone hurts you, but it can help you in the process of forgiveness. These methods have helped me, and I truly believe they will help you.

You cannot wait until you feel warm and loving toward someone who hurt you to forgive them. You'll probably have to do it while you are still hurting and forgiving is the last thing you feel like doing, but doing it puts you in the "God league." It puts you squarely on the road that is "narrow (contracted by pressure)," but leads to the way of life (Matt. 7:14). It puts you on the road less traveled, the one that Jesus Himself traveled on. Don't forget that one of the last things He did was forgive someone who didn't deserve forgiveness, and He did it while hanging on a cross being crucified. I think some of the last things that Jesus did were specially designed to help us remember how important those things are.

If someone hurts you, cry a river, then build a bridge and get over it.
Unknown

If someone hurts you, cry a river, then
build a bridge and get over it.
Unknown

What If I Decide It's Just Too Hard?

Many people decide that forgiving those who have hurt them is just too hard, and indeed, forgiving is hard! But in making the decision not to forgive, they are making one of the most serious mistakes they can possibly make. Why is it so serious? Because our intimacy with God is hindered if we won't forgive those who have sinned against us. The Bible clearly says that if we don't forgive others, God will not forgive us our sins and iniquities (see Matt. 6:14–15). If our sin stands between God and us, then we will find it difficult to hear from Him and to feel His presence. I firmly believe that harboring unforgiveness steals our sleep, our peace, and our joy. It affects our health and adversely robs us of our well-being in general. Show me someone who doesn't have a forgiving spirit, and I'll show you someone whom very few people want to be around.

Sometimes we have harbored resentment for so long that we don't even realize we have it. It has become part of us— and that is really dangerous.

I can remember thinking at one time that I had no unforgiveness at all in my heart, but God showed me two specific things that surprised me: I was angry at one of my daughter's friends because I did not like the way she treated my daughter, and I was also angry toward my son because he just wasn't what I wanted him to be at the time.

Have you ever felt angry toward someone you loved because the choices they made in life disappointed you or didn't meet your expectations? I am sure you have, because this is one of Satan's more subtle traps. We are not angry over something the person did to us but something they did not do. We disapprove of their choices, even though God has given them the right to make them. We may try to encourage those we love and care about, but we must not try to control them. God tells us to train up our children in the way they should go, not the way we want them to go (see Prov. 22:6).

Barbara had five children she loved very much. They were all grown and all but one had children of their own. Although Barbara was a knowledgeable Christian, she had difficulty letting her children make their own choices. Quite frequently her behavior sparked arguments between her and her children. They felt controlled and manipulated, but she insisted she was only trying to help them. Their anger would hurt Barbara's feelings, and Barbara's behavior would make them angry. The result was a vicious cycle that made all of them unhappy. Barbara didn't realize it, but actually she behaved the same way with most of the people she knew. As a result, people began to avoid her.

Barbara attended church and a Bible study group, but sadly she never stopped making unloving comments about other people's choices and decisions. She was a type of Christian described as "carnal," which I mentioned earlier in the book. She believed in God but never stopped doing what she felt like doing. Sadly, she ended up with very few friends, a husband who left her for another woman, and children who avoided her whenever possible. The root of her problem was pride. She believed that her way was right for everyone and that she was just trying to help people, even though they truly did not want her help.

I felt angry toward my son because he wasn't as spiritual as I wanted him to be, but I was wrong, and through God I found the strength to tell him that I was. The humility God enabled me to show in saying, "I was wrong," and the unconditional acceptance of him as he was, started a healing in his life that eventually helped him make right decisions and get on the right road. Prior to that time, he had felt my disapproval, and all it did was drive the wedge between us deeper and deeper.

I have discovered that sometimes when I'm hurt, it's not because of something another person did to hurt me; it's because I had an expectation that I shouldn't have had. There are of course things we have a right to expect in our relationships with other people, but we must make sure that our expectations are realistic and that they still give people the freedom to be themselves.

It's Time to Make a Decision

Nothing changes in our lives until we make a decision to act on the information we have. Here are a few decisions you can make that will enable you to live free of the agony of bitterness, resentment, and unforgiveness:

1. Believe the best of every person. Give them the benefit of the doubt.
2. Imitate Jesus in showing mercy to people.
3. Understand that hurting people hurt people, and pray for those who hurt you.
4. Don't let your emotions make your decisions.
5. Remember that if you make right choices, your emotions will eventually come in line with your decisions.
6. You have God's power to enable you to do difficult things.

7. Refusing to forgive is like taking poison and hoping it will get rid of your enemy.
8. God expects us to give away what we have freely received from Him—including forgiveness.
9. Forgiveness = freedom. Don't become your own jailer!
10. Don't ever waste another day being bitter. Each day is a gift from God—use it wisely.

I believe that Satan uses unforgiveness to bring destruction into our lives. God tells us again and again in His Word how important it is to forgive. I believe it is foolish to disobey God in this area. I plan to work with the Holy Spirit every day of my life to resist letting my emotions prevent me from forgiving those who hurt or disappoint me. I will not let Satan control my destiny! I pray you will make the same decision.

Decision and confession: *I will quickly and freely forgive those who hurt me. I refuse to ruin my life with bitterness.*

CHAPTER
17

How Emotions Affect Our Health

Millions of people simply don't take good care of themselves. They invest in everything imaginable except themselves. I believe God gives us an allotted amount of energy for our lives, and if we use it all up in the first forty years, we will probably experience lots of health issues later in life. In *Look Great, Feel Great*, I share my own journey of doing it all wrong in the hope that I can help others avoid the mistakes I made.

Excessive stress over a long period of time negatively affects our health and emotions. We have heard endless times how we need to eliminate unnecessary stress from our lives, yet most people never do it until they have a health crisis.

When I don't feel well, I find that it's much more difficult to be stable emotionally. I recently returned from a conference that was the culmination of three weeks of travel and hard work. I was very tired but wanted to see all my children, so we invited them and their families to meet us for lunch as soon as we got back home. Twelve of them were able to come, and although getting together with them sounded like a great idea at the time, it turned out to be the straw that broke the camel's back. The restaurant was very noisy, so we had to talk loud in order to be heard—hardly relaxing. Then someone brought up a situation that had caused a lot of trouble in our lives. You probably know what I mean when I say, *I just didn't want to hear anything else about it, and especially not when I was tired.* The more they discussed it back and forth, the more emotional I felt. I thought, *If they don't shut up, I am going to scream!* Ordinarily, none of this would have bothered me, but because I was so tired, anything that even sounded remotely negative or sad was almost more than I could handle. *I wanted to hear happy things!*

My two sons were teasing me, as they often do, and usually we have a lot of fun with it. But because I was tired, most of what they said came across as insulting. I took offense, even though they weren't trying to offend me, simply because I was exhausted. On that particular day I *felt* like I wanted everyone in my family to give me compliments, tell me how they appreciated all my hard work, tell me how much they loved me, and perhaps even pay for my dinner. But none of that happened, and by the time I left, I was a borderline basket case. My thoughts were in the sewer, and my emotions were paying a visit to the pity-parlor where I once lived. It was clearly one of those situations where my own expectations had caused the problem. I had an expectation that my family did not even know I had, and when they failed to meet it, I became emotional. Thankfully, I was able to get out of the restaurant before my children realized I was deteriorating rapidly.

I could have avoided the whole scene by simply having

a quick and quiet dinner with Dave. But I let the enemy in through a lack of wisdom, and the entire rest of the evening and even most of the next day was a game of me trying to keep my emotions under control, and I have to say that I was not totally successful. I am certainly glad that the Bible says we have a High Priest (Jesus) who understands us because He was tempted in all respects just like us, yet He never sinned. He was in total control of His emotions, but He still understands us; therefore, we can boldly approach His throne of grace and receive the help we need even though we behave less than perfectly (see Heb. 4:15–16).

We got home after the dinner fiasco, and within thirty minutes our electricity went out due to a storm. For the rest of the evening, we were in the dark except for candles. My plan for rest, relaxation, and a good movie was failing in front of my eyes, and there was nothing I could do about it. I ended up going to bed at 6:00 p.m., which was not very exciting after having worked all weekend.

I woke up the next morning in a sad, weepy, self-pitying mood and spent my time with God crying and moaning about my woes. I did stop at regular intervals to tell God that I knew how very blessed I was, and I knew I was acting ridiculous, but I was so tired that I didn't even have the energy to resist. I suggest that you stop for a moment and think about how you feel, think, talk, and behave when you are extremely tired or sick. If we don't face the truth about where we are in our behavior and spiritual maturity, we can never get to where we need to be!

I knew that I needed quiet, rest, and a good, hot meal. I also needed a cookie and a new pair of shoes! (If you have no idea why I made that statement, then you need to read my book *Eat the Cookie... Buy the Shoes*, which talks about how we need to make an investment in ourselves and reward ourselves for our successes in life.)

I had just successfully completed three weeks of hard work, and I needed to celebrate. We all want to be rewarded for our hard work, and it is very wise to do something for yourself that you enjoy as part of your restoration program. When Dave is tired, he likes to play golf or watch a baseball game, and doing so actually energizes him. I need rest, a good meal, a dessert, and a good movie. One of the most important things I need after a hectic schedule with tons of people around all the time is to simply be quiet. I did not need to plan another party in a noisy restaurant with lots of people the moment I returned home. It was my fault and no one else's. I have enough knowledge and experience to know better, but knowing what we should do is one thing and applying what we know is quite another.

Are You Ignoring Warnings?

I believe God has designed our bodies in such a way that they often warn us when something is going wrong before it gets really bad. This warning is our opportunity to take some positive action and prevent a major crisis. If you have children, you've probably said thousands of times, "I'm warning you, if you keep doing that, you're going to be in big trouble." We are giving them an opportunity to make a change before they have to suffer. I believe our bodies are built in such a marvelous way that they give us the same opportunity. Have you ever had pain in an area like your neck, back, or shoulder and let it go until suddenly you had a major problem? I know I have, and I have done just that (let it go) more than once. I have also watched other people do it time and again. If you hear yourself or someone you love talking regularly about an area of her body that hurts, then that is a warning sign that something needs to be checked.

For years my feet hurt after my conferences. Sometimes they hurt so badly I could have cried. I rubbed them, soaked them, and used a variety of cooling foot rubs on them. Then I got up the next morning, put on high-heeled shoes, and persecuted my feet again all day. I had worn high heels for many years. I love pretty shoes, so I opted for cute instead of comfort. It was unwise, and I eventually paid the price for it. I define *wisdom* as "doing now what you will be satisfied with later on." I did what I liked at the moment and suffered for it later on. Furthermore, I did it for years and eventually developed bunions and corns that required surgery.

My feet got better, and I did start wearing shoes with lower heels, but only a little lower. It helped, but my back started giving me trouble. So I ignored that—until I woke up one morning and couldn't walk without assistance. That day I began going to the chiropractor and have visited him regularly ever since. I finally started a workout and exercise program with a trainer so I wouldn't hurt myself even more, and that has helped a lot. But over the years that I ignored the pain in my back, I was systematically damaging it. My body was warning me to do something *now*, but I put it off.

By now you may be thinking, *Joyce, you are not very smart.*

Before you judge me, let me ask you what you're ignoring. Are you tired all the time? Do you have pain in your head, neck, shoulders, back, hips, knees, or feet and the only action you take is to complain? Is your blood pressure high, but you do nothing to lower your stress? Is your blood sugar high, but you keep eating lots of sweets?

When the gas gauge says your automobile is low on fuel, you don't ignore it. And if you do, you end up on the side of the road with no gas and no transportation. If your oil gauge says your car is low on oil, then you add oil. My car has a "brain." It is some kind of fancy computer that does lots of things I really couldn't care less about. Two weeks ago it went crazy and believe me, I paid attention to it quick. I got all kinds of messages on the dashboard gadgets that sounded really scary. In fact, I refused to drive it another mile until it was fixed because I was not going to take a chance of being out somewhere and having it break down. If we respected the warnings we get from our bodies the way we do the ones from our cars, we would be a lot healthier.

If you don't feel well, there is a possibility that you are grouchy, easily offended, and excusing all your bad behavior by saying, "I don't feel well." Ask yourself, *Are there some things I can do that could change this situation or at least help it?* I believe if we do what we can do, then God will do what we cannot do. When we are sick, we pray and ask for help and healing from God, but are we doing what we can do to keep ourselves healthy? Sometimes when we ask God for help, He tries to show us something we are doing that is causing our problems, but we don't want to change anything—we just want the pain or exhaustion to go away. Wisdom knows that if we need a change, we will not get it by continuing to do the same things we have always done.

It is amazing how much better you might feel if you do some simple things like eat healthier, drink plenty of water, get adequate rest, balance out your work with rest, and laugh, laugh, laugh.

The Mirth Diet

It is scientifically proven that laughter improves our health, and if it improves our health, our moods will be better.

A happy heart is good medicine and a cheerful mind works healing, but a broken spirit dries up the bones. (*Proverbs 17:22*)

Did you know that it takes a lot more muscles to frown than it does to smile? One website said it takes four muscles to smile and sixty-four to frown. I think I will save muscle energy and start smiling more! When we laugh it stimulates the parts of our brain that use the "feel good" chemical, dopamine. The immune system is triggered, and laughter even seems to help diabetics keep their glucose levels in check.

Researchers at the University of Maryland learned that when we laugh, the inner lining of our blood vessels expands, and "good" chemicals are produced that reduce clotting and inflammation. When the blood vessel linings contract, stress hormones (cortisol) are released. A hearty laugh tenses all your muscles for seconds or minutes at a time, and your heart rate and blood pressure go up while you laugh and fall below your baseline afterward, just like exercising. I have heard that laughter is equivalent to internal jogging.

People who are happier in their daily lives have healthier levels of key chemicals than those who are unhappy. A study in England showed that the happier people are, the lower their levels of cortisol are, which is linked to diabetes and heart disease. A Carnegie Mellon University study confirmed that people who are happy, lively, calm, or exhibit other positive emotions are less likely to become ill when they are exposed to a cold virus than those who report few of these emotions.

This research states that laughter increases good health, and I believe that both of those things help us be more stable emotionally. So why not laugh, laugh, and laugh some more?!

Dave has enjoyed extremely good health in his seventy years of life, and he has exercised for fifty years and has a knack for enjoying everything. I noticed just this morning that within the first hour we were up, he found humor in at least ten things. They were simple things that a more intense person would not have found funny at all, but Dave did. His silliness made me laugh, and that is good for me because I am a more serious-minded individual—especially when I have work to do.

Try it! You can even make it a game to see how often you can laugh in one day, and I believe it will help relieve tension that in turn will help your overall health and emotions. Are you an intense person who stresses over things that wouldn't make any difference at all to you if you knew this was your last day on earth? If I had one day left, I would certainly want to enjoy it, wouldn't you?

More than likely some of my readers are thinking, *Joyce,*

I just don't have anything to laugh about. My life is a mess and I have problems everywhere I look. That may be true, but I believe we can find some humor in almost everything if we are determined to do so. I realize there are tragic things that happen, like terminal disease or the death of a loved one, and I am not suggesting there is anything humorous about those things. The Bible says that there's a time to laugh and a time to weep and mourn (see Eccl. 3:4). Trying to be funny at the wrong time can be hurtful to people who are already hurting. However, I strongly suggest that we all find as much humor as we can in everything we can, as often as we can. If we do, then even the more difficult and tragic times in life will be easier to handle. We don't laugh at our problems, but in spite of them. The Bible says that the joy of the Lord is our strength (see Neh. 8:10), and we would do well to remember that.

> Joy, temperance and repose
> slam the door on the doctor's nose.
> *Henry Wadsworth Longfellow*

Controlling Emotions When You're Sick

It is definitely more difficult to manage your emotions when you are sick or exhausted, but it is not impossible. When feeling bad is a once-a-month event, I tell women to get extra rest, avoid making big decisions, and say as little as possible. But what if a serious illness is involved? Diet changes, exercise, laughing, and some of the other things I have suggested won't change a thing for people who are very sick and need healing.

During the waiting time, whether you're waiting for the doctor, waiting to get a prescription, or waiting for a miracle from God, you have to deal with life. I have noticed that things don't stop happening just because I don't feel like dealing with them.

Can you manage your emotions during these times? Absolutely! It will be more difficult, it may require extra prayer and more determination, but you can do it with God's help. The first step toward being able to manage your emotions during times like this is to believe that you can. If we could not remain stable in every kind of situation, then God's Word would say, "Be stable, except when you feel bad." It doesn't say that, but rather we are taught to remain stable during every storm of life. It has helped me immensely to learn that God will give me the ability to do anything I have to do if I trust Him and spend lots of time with Him.

Psalm 91:1 teaches that if we dwell in the secret place of the Most High, we will remain "stable and fixed under the shadow of the Almighty [Whose power no foe can withstand]." That means if we spend lots of time in God's presence, waiting on Him, praying and meditating on His Word, then we will receive the strength we need to accomplish whatever we need to do.

The first mistake we often make is listening to the "this is just too hard" lie. Satan is a liar, and he always puts thoughts into our minds that say we are not capable, can't, won't, and never will be able to. The devil is a glass-half-empty guy, but God always sees the glass as full and overflowing. We can choose to adopt God's attitude and be an "I think I can" person, instead of an "I think I can't" person. If you believe you can remain stable and control your emotions even during times in which it is difficult to do so, then you will find God working through your faith and enabling you to do what you believed.

I know people who have been sick for an extended period of time and have the most beautiful attitudes. They never complain, are not grouchy, don't act as if the world owes them something, and they don't blame God or even feel sorry for themselves. But I also know people with the same circumstance who talk only about their illnesses, medical appointments, and how hard it all is for them. They are easily offended, bitter, and resentful. Every situation in life requires making a decision about how we are going to respond, and if we respond the way God would, then our trials are much easier to handle. I highly respect and admire people who are able to be stable even when they are in tremendous pain and discomfort. I think they are a wonderful example to all of us.

I am going to quote a scripture that you have probably heard hundreds of times, but this time I am asking you to look at each word and really think about what it is saying:

I have strength for all things in Christ Who empowers me [I am ready for anything and equal to anything through Him Who infuses inner strength into me; I am self-sufficient in Christ's sufficiency]. (*Philippians 4:13*)

Wow! What an encouraging verse that is. We don't have to be afraid of upcoming things, we don't have to dread them, and we don't have to let circumstances defeat us before we even try to conquer them. God is on our side, and His grace is sufficient to meet our every need.

Perhaps you have never even thought about how important it is to manage your emotions during times of crisis. I imagine we all think, *I can't help how I act right now; I am having a hard time, and that is all there is to it.* That is a normal human reaction, but with God on our side helping us, we don't have to behave the way a "normal" person would. Satan is our enemy, and his goal is to get us so emotionally rattled that we start saying a lot of things that will provide him with an opening into our lives. Or he hopes we will make a lot of unwise decisions during painful times and create messes that we will have to deal with for a long, long time afterward.

The apostle Paul, inspired by the Holy Spirit, wrote in Philippians that we should not even for one moment be frightened or intimidated by anything our opponents and adversaries would heap on us. He said that our fearlessness and constancy would be a sign to our enemies of their impending destruction, and a token and evidence of our deliverance and salvation from God (see Phil. 1:28). In other words, it seems that when we have trials, the spiritual world is watching. God is watching and Satan is watching, and how we respond and what we say and do are *very* important. I have believed for years that if I can hold my tongue and remain emotionally stable during times of difficulty, then I am honoring God and letting the devil know he is not going to control me.

I'm not always successful, but I'm certainly a lot better than I once was. As I often say, "I am not where I need to be, but thank God I am not where I used to be." I am still growing, but at least I've learned the importance of managing my emotions, and I hope you are also seeing how important it is to do that.

There is no doubt that it is more difficult to manage your

emotions when you're sick, but hopefully you are learning that it is an option.

Don't Deny Emotions, Just Control Them

It is important to me that you understand I am not saying to deny your emotions exist, but deny them the right to control you. We all have loads of feelings about hundreds if not thousands of different things. As I said, it seems that emotions have a mind of their own. If your health is not good, your emotions may possibly scream louder than normal, and that is to be expected. Pain is not easy to deal with. Being told by medical professionals that you have a disease is not a fun thing. I know because I've had my share of times like that, but I have discovered it is much easier on me if I don't let my emotions go wild. The more you stay in control of your emotions, the better your decisions will be.

Out-of-control emotions wear me out, and I am sure they affect you the same way. Anger makes me tired; guilt makes me tired; frustration and wild thoughts all make me tired. I even get exhausted if I talk all day about problems and negative things. The very fact that these things drain us should be proof that they steal from us rather than add to our overall wellness. The next time you hear bad news of any kind and feel yourself starting to get upset or discouraged, remember this book and the principles I am sharing, then make a decision to remain calm and ask God to give you direction.

Decision and confession: *When I am tired or sick, I will manage my emotions and not allow them to control me.*

CHAPTER

18

Stress and Emotions

We cannot avoid all stress, and in fact some stress is good and necessary. But too much stress affects us very negatively. It contributes immensely to emotional outbursts that are not good for us or the people around us.

The word *stress* was originally an engineering term. It referred to how much pressure a building could take before it collapsed. These days a lot more people are collapsing from stress than buildings. We reinforce our buildings so they can withstand storms, hurricanes, earthquakes, and other such things, but what are we doing to make sure we don't collapse in our own storms, hurricanes, and earthquake-size problems?

Do you feel and think, *I am stressed to the point of breaking*, and yet you do nothing about it? I pray that after reading this chapter, you will make some decisions that will relieve a lot of the pressure you are under. Very often our stress and pressure are due to the fact that we have committed to too many things. If you have said, "I don't know why I feel so frustrated all the time," it would be a good idea to have one of those meetings with yourself that I have talked about and take a serious look at what you are doing and, most importantly, *why* you are doing what you do.

Here is the short version of what happens in your body when you experience stress.

The state of upset or arousal sets off a natural alarm in our bodies, called the "fight-or-flight" response, designed to help us defend ourselves against threatening hostile events. Even thinking of an upsetting event or imagining danger can also set off the alarm. So that means thinking about things that give us stress can cause the same reaction as if we were actually experiencing the stressful event.

The brain, pituitary gland, adrenal gland, and adrenal cortex tell the body to make cortisol. Cortisol fights inflammation, and it increases blood sugar and muscle tension. Adrenaline is also produced, which increases the heart rate, raises blood pressure and cholesterol levels, and sends glucose to muscles. All these responses are helping us deal with the stressful event or emergency we are facing. It is marvelous that God has created our bodies in such a way that they do these things for us. Actually, our bodies want to help us!

But the same reactions to stress that are built into our bodies to help us will actually harm us if we allow stress to cause this fight-or-flight response to be repeated excessively. Just think of a rubber band. It stretches, but if it is stretched too far or too often, it can break. I've tied knots in them and kept using them until I had a rubber band with four knots, but eventually it wore out; it had just been stretched too far too many times. God brought this to mind as an example of how we treat our bodies when it comes to stress. We stretch ourselves until something breaks, then we put a bandage on it by medicating the symptom. We just keep doing the same thing until something else breaks and we repeat the process. We eventually feel like that rubber band with the four knots tied in it to hold it together. I have even said, "I have had so much stress lately that I feel like I am all tied up in knots." What I meant was that I had run in high gear for so long that I felt like I couldn't relax. I was aching, tense, tired, and had indigestion and heartburn, just to name a few knots.

What Will It Take to Get Us to Change?

Sadly, we normally don't change until a crisis forces us to. You may think as I did, *I can't do anything about my life because I really do have to do everything I am doing.* I can tell you from experience that is absolutely not true. God never gives us more than we can do with peace and joy. I did a lot of what I did because I wanted to do it. I had myself convinced I *had* to, but the truth was that I *wanted* to.

Perhaps you are one of those rare people who have a lot of balance in their lives, and you use a lot of wisdom. But if you aren't, then please don't waste most of your life before you make the changes that can help you enjoy it. "The executive who works from 7:00 a.m. to 7:00 p.m. every day will be both successful and fondly remembered by his wife's next husband," author John Capozzi wrote. That is a statement worth thinking about. The writer of Ecclesiastes said, "I hated life, because what is done under the sun was grievous to me; for all is vanity and a striving after the wind and a feeding on it. And I hated all my labor in which I had toiled under the sun, seeing that I must leave it to the man who will succeed me" (Eccl. 2:17–18). I think when Solomon wrote that, he was having a bad day. He may have been depressed and discouraged because he was worn-out from trying to obtain and maintain so much stuff. Later in chapter 2, he said something wise: "There is nothing better for a man than that he should eat and drink and make himself enjoy good in his labor. Even this, I have seen, is from the hand of God" (v. 24). How many people do you know who work too hard, are committed to a lot more than they can handle peacefully, and never really seem to enjoy any of it? Are you one of those people? If so, what will it take to get you to change?

> Stress is an ignorant state. It believes
> that everything is an emergency.
> *Natalie Goldberg*

When people die, someone usually asks, "I wonder how much he left?" The answer is that he left it all. Everyone does. You and I will never have this moment again, so we should make every effort to enjoy it.

Stress management is a multibillion-dollar business, and you've probably read a book or an article (or several if you're desperate enough) on how to get your life under control. I doubt any of us manage our lives well unless we are led by the Spirit of God, and that means we follow wisdom and peace. I have finally admitted I am not smart enough to run my own life well without help from God. Someone saw a billboard that read "If you want to make me laugh, tell me your plans." It was signed "God"!

> *Someone saw a billboard that read "If you want to make me laugh, tell me your plans." It was signed "God"!*

We may be good at making plans, but without considering wisdom, peace, and the need for balance. We also tend to forget all the other things we have already committed to until it is too late and we are worn-out and frustrated.

Why Can't I Relax and Enjoy My Life?

People who are tired and worn-out, uptight and irritated, usually spend a lot of time complaining about it, but they do little or nothing to change it. They want to understand why they feel the way they feel, but even if someone told them, they still probably wouldn't change a thing. We feel trapped! We actually think we *have* to do all the things we do, but the truth is that we don't. If you got sick and had to be hospitalized for a month, life would go on. Either someone else would do what you were doing, or—shockingly—it might just not get done at all, with no adverse reaction.

I am not suggesting we ignore our responsibilities, but I do believe we need to learn that we cannot do everything we want to do, or everything everyone else wants us to do. The first key to lowering your stress level is to learn to say no. We cannot be people-pleasers and keep stress at a manageable level.

We cannot even do everything everyone else does. Some people are able to accomplish more than others, but we must learn to live within our own limits.

Everyone has limits, but they are not all the same. I make very fast decisions, but I know other people who need more time to make decisions and that is fine. I also have an unusual amount of endurance. These abilities are God's grace enabling me to do what He has given me to do.

I had an assistant who tried to keep up with me, and she seemed to be doing great and loved it all. But she ended up almost collapsing mentally, emotionally, and physically. She wanted to please me so much that she wasn't honest with me about her limits. I can sometimes expect too much out of people because I can accomplish a lot, but it is not my fault if they don't communicate with me about what they feel they can do and be healthy and happy. Quite often people don't communicate honestly with their employers because they fear they might lose their jobs. But, even if that were the case, they would be far better off to lose the job and get another one instead of being stressed out all the time.

One of our biggest stressors in life can be comparing ourselves to and competing with other people. The good news is that you are free to be yourself. You don't need to ever try to be someone else.

Stress Feeds Anxiety

Nothing harms us emotionally the way stress does. We might say that anxiety is emotions out of control. When someone experiences anxiety most of the time, it's because their emotions have been pressured to the point that they are no longer functioning healthily. There are many situations that cause anxiety. The death of a spouse or child, divorce, and job loss are major events; however, not all the reasons are that serious. A lot of anxiety is caused simply by taking on more than we can handle.

There is no answer for emotional distress unless we learn to follow God's principles of wisdom. I used to feel like I was going crazy due to stress, but it was because my schedule was insane. And—even worse—I thought I was doing it for God. It is amazing to me now when I look back how deceived I was. Always remember that if Satan cannot get you to not work for God, then he will try to get you to overwork for God. He really doesn't care which end of being out of balance we are on, because either one causes trouble.

I could write an entire book on this subject, but the simple answer to living a life you can enjoy is to learn God's ways and follow them. Jesus said, "I am the Way" (John 14:6), and that means He will show us how to live properly. The answers we need are in the Bible, and we should make a decision that we will not only read it, but we will obey it. If we refuse to make that decision and follow through, we will keep feeling stressed until we break. I am sure that some of you have decided while reading this book that there are many changes you need to make in order to get your emotions under control. Don't put those changes off until you've forgotten about them, because procrastination is one of the devil's best weapons. Take action. You don't even have to finish the book before you get started. You can start while you are still reading. As a matter of fact, I am challenging you to make one decision today and put it into action. Do it as a seed of your commitment to get your emotions under control.

Perhaps you were hoping I would give you three easy steps to removing excess stress and enjoying emotional stability. I am sorry to disappoint you, but anything worth having is worth making an effort to obtain. I can say with all honesty that at one time I was extremely out of balance and very stressed. I also let my emotions control me; but I have changed, and so can you. Start asking God what you can eliminate from your life that is not producing good fruit. It may even be some good things that are just not the best things for you. Something can be right for us in one season of our lives and not right at all in another season. Don't be afraid to tell people that you have to stop doing something. Follow God! Follow peace! Follow your heart, and you will accomplish a lot of fruitful things and still have energy left over to enjoy the fruit of your labor.

As I close this chapter, let me leave you with these words from Jesus:

Peace I leave with you; My [own] peace I now give and bequeath to you. Not as the world gives do I give to you. Do not let your hearts be troubled, neither let them be afraid. [Stop allowing yourselves to be agitated and disturbed; and do not permit yourselves to be fearful and intimidated and cowardly and unsettled.]   (*John 14:27*)

It is obvious from Jesus' words that He desires for us to have wonderful peace, but please notice that He is also giving us a responsibility. We must control the negative emotions that would steal our peace. We cannot always control all our circumstances, but we can control ourselves with God's help.

> *Peace I leave with you; My [own] peace I now give and bequeath to you. Not as the world gives do I give to you. Do not let your hearts be troubled, neither let them be afraid. [Stop allowing yourselves to be agitated and disturbed; and do not permit yourselves to be fearful and intimidated and cowardly and unsettled.]*
> John 14:27

Decision and confession: *I will live with peace and not do more than I can handle.*

CHAPTER
19

Good Emotions

We tend to focus on emotions that are troublesome, but there are many emotions that are good—emotions that promote health, contentment, joy, productivity, and a sense of well-being. Without those emotions, it would be a dull, dull world. Yes, many emotions need to be managed, but many of them can be a source of enjoyment. The first example of a positive emotion that comes to mind is happiness. I believe the main thing everyone wants in life is to be happy. No matter what our pursuits are, we hope they bring us happiness.

If a person works hard to accomplish goals, she does it because it makes her feel happy. My daughter Sandra is a highly organized woman. She told me once that when she can check everything off her list as being done, it makes her feel really happy. Frequently when we talk by phone and I ask her what she is doing, she says, "Organizing." I am a little different from my daughter. I love for things to be organized, but I prefer not to be the one who organizes them.

My assistant is good at organizing. I can give her a pile of all kinds of stuff and say, "Get this organized somewhere so I can actually look on a shelf and see what I have." I pay her to organize so I can be happy.

I believe things being well organized gives us a sense of order and peace, and that produces a sense of calm as well as happiness. Chaos, on the other hand, leaves us confused and unhappy. God is a God of order, not confusion. If your surroundings are chaotic, I'd venture to guess that other parts of your life are out of order too. I suggest you get organized. If you just can't seem to do it yourself, you might pay someone to do it, or find a friend or relative who actually loves the task of organizing and ask them for help. You can "barter" with them and in turn help them with something you're especially good at.

What do you do that makes you happy? People go on vacations hoping to buy a little happiness. Sometimes they even go into debt to buy a week's worth of happiness, and then when the bills come in, they aren't happy anymore. Some of the things we purchase are needs, but many are just things we think will make us happy. People worldwide stand at merchandise counters right now, waiting to pay for something they think or hope will make them happy.

We get married hoping it will make us happy, and after a while some get divorced hoping it will make them happy. People often change jobs searching for happiness. We even do things we don't like doing, just so we can be happy with the end result. A woman may not like to clean house, but she looks at her clean house and feels happy, so week after week she cleans it. Actually, I cannot think of anything we do that does not have happiness as a motivator. There are many things that make me happy, but I have found that obeying God is the number one thing that makes me happy. When I am flowing with God I have a deep contentment that nothing else compares to. I may not always like what He asks me to do or not to do, but if I resist and rebel, I will not be happy down deep in my soul; and if I obey, I will be happy.

Sadly, many people don't obey God and then frantically wear themselves out trying to get or buy happiness some other way. No matter what we own, we will not be happy if doing God's will is not a priority in our lives.

Why Are So Many Christians Unhappy?

I think some people have a perception that Christianity is stern, severe, and joyless. That's because many who call themselves Christians have sour attitudes and sad faces. They are critical of others and quick to judge. Those of us who love and serve God and His Son, Jesus Christ, should be the happiest people on earth. We should be able to enjoy everything we do, simply because we know that God is present. It was a great day for me when I finally discovered through studying the Bible that *God wants us to enjoy our lives*. In fact, He sent Jesus to ensure that we would be able to (see John 10:10). Our joy makes God happy!

Happiness is an emotion that fosters well-being, and I believe it is contagious. One of the best ways to witness to others about Jesus is to be happy and enjoy all that we do. Since everyone simply wants to be happy, if they see that being a Christian will produce happiness, they will be open to learning about and receiving Jesus themselves.

There are many emotions we have to resist, but happiness is not one of them! So go ahead and be as happy as you can possibly be.

I Feel Excited

Excitement, zeal, and passion are also positive emotions. They energize us to press forward in our pursuits. The Bible instructs us to be zealous and enthusiastic as we serve the Lord (see Rom. 12:11). In Revelation 3:19, God instructs us to even be enthusiastic and burning with zeal when He chastises or corrects us. Why should we do that? Simply because He expects us to trust that everything He does is for our ultimate good.

I make a point of trying to be excited about each day that God gives me. The psalmist David said this: "This is the day which the Lord has brought about; we will rejoice and be glad in it" (Psalm 118:24). Good emotions come from good decisions and good thoughts. For years I got up each day and waited to see how I felt, then I let those feelings dictate the course of my day. Now, I set my mind in the right direction and make decisions that I know will produce emotions I can enjoy.

I wasted enough years of my life letting

> *For years I got up each day and waited to see how I felt, then I let those feelings dictate the course of my day. Now, I set my mind in the right direction and make decisions that I know will produce emotions I can enjoy.*

negative and even poisonous emotions control me, and I refuse to do it any longer. Each day I decide to enjoy the day, to be excited about whatever I do and do it with zeal and enthusiasm. I make a decision every day to be content! I won't be able to carry out my decision if I don't set my mind and keep it set in the right direction. I firmly believe that feelings follow decisions.

Living Ordinary Days with an Extraordinary Attitude

Most of our days are rather ordinary. We all have moments in life that are amazing, but a lot of life is Monday, Tuesday, Wednesday, Thursday, Friday, Saturday, Sunday, and back to Monday all over again. Two weeks ago I stood in front of 225,000 people in Zimbabwe preaching the Gospel of Jesus Christ and teaching the Word of God. It was my birthday, and 225,000 people sang "Happy Birthday" to me and that was rather cool. Yesterday I went to the Target store to buy new kitchen rugs and then to the grocery store, but I can honestly say that I enjoyed Zimbabwe and the grocery store equally. Zimbabwe was a once-in-a-lifetime event that was exciting, and one I will never forget, but having another day to enjoy God is also exciting, even if the day is spent doing errands. God's presence makes life exciting if we have a proper understanding of life as a whole. Everything we do is sacred if we do it unto the Lord and we believe that He is with us. Ask yourself right now if you truly believe that God is with you. If your answer is yes, just think about how amazing that is, and my guess is that your enjoyment will increase immediately.

I believe the psalmist David discovered the secret to enthusiasm. He simply decided and declared, "This is the day the Lord has made, I will rejoice and be glad in it." The "I will" says it all. He made a decision that produced the feelings he wanted rather than waiting to see how he felt.

The Value of Optimism

Optimism is an attitude we can adopt that will produce anticipation and joy. Living with positive expectation is a lovely thing. Optimism takes a very gray day and paints it with beautiful color. Anticipation and expectation wait with an attitude that something good is about to happen at any moment. What are you expecting today and tomorrow, or, for that matter, what are you expecting out of life? The psalmist David said that he did not know what would have become of him had he not believed that he would see the Lord's goodness while he was still alive (see Psalm 27:13).

The feeling or emotion of anticipation is good, so go ahead and expect God to show Himself strong on your behalf. Anticipation is the opposite of hopelessness, and I personally believe hopelessness is the worst feeling in the world. We have to have a reason to get up each day. Hopeless people become depressed. Everything in their lives seems dark and gloomy. God wants us to live in Technicolor. His desire is to be good to us, but we must be expecting His goodness in faith. Some people might think it humble to expect nothing, but I think it is unbiblical. We don't deserve anything, but God is good and kind and He wants to give us good things anyway. Isaiah 30:18 states that God is looking to be gracious, to have mercy and show loving-kindness, and those who wait for Him to do that are blessed indeed. What are you waiting for? Are you a "get out of bed and see what happens" person? Or do you get up each day with an optimistic view of anticipation, expectation, and joy?

Relax and Go with the Flow

A feeling of being relaxed is wonderful. Being nervous, tense, and worried is not wonderful, so why aren't more people relaxed? Jesus said if we are weary and overburdened, we should go to Him and He will give us rest, relaxation, and ease (see Matt. 11:28–29). Jesus wants to teach us the right way to live, which is different from the way most of the world lives.

It would be putting it mildly to say that I was an uptight woman for the first half of my life. I simply did not know how to relax, and it was due to my not being willing to completely trust God. I trusted God *for* things, but not *in* things. I kept trying to be the one in control. Even though God was in the driver's seat of my life, I kept one hand on the wheel just in case He took a wrong turn. Relaxation is impossible without trust! Dave is the most relaxed individual I have ever met. Part of it may be his God-given temperament, but most of it is his faith in God. Dave truly believes that no matter what happens in our lives, God will take care of it, and that enables him to relax.

We have even discovered that God can and will fix our

mistakes and make them work for our good if we keep praying and trusting Him. All things are possible with God. If you know you can't fix the problem you have, then why not relax while God is working on it? It sounds easy, but it took many years for me to be able to do this. I know from experience that the ability to relax and go with the flow in life is dependent upon our willingness to trust God *completely*.

If things don't go your way, instead of being upset, you can believe that getting your way was not what you needed. God knew that, so He gave you what was best for you, instead of what you wanted. The minute you do that, your soul and body relax, and you will be able to enjoy life.

If you are waiting much longer than you had hoped to in some situation, you can get frustrated, angry, and upset, or you can say, "God's timing is perfect; He is never late. And my steps are ordered by the Lord." Now you can relax and simply go with the flow of what is happening in your life. Of course there are things we need to resist, such as evil and the temptation to behave in an ungodly way. But when it comes to things that are out of our control, we can either ruin the day or relax and enjoy it while God is working on the situation. As long as we believe, God keeps working!

Closeness and Detachment

I believe we are created for connection. God wants us to be able to connect with and feel close to other people, which is one of the great joys of life. Sadly, it can also be a source of pain, making it easy to become aloof and detached. We think we are protecting ourselves, but the pain of loneliness and isolation is much worse than the pain of relationship.

I did not trust anyone after fifteen years of being sexually abused by my father and experiencing unfaithfulness from my husband in my first marriage. My motto was, "If you don't let anyone into your life, they cannot hurt you." It seemed to work for a while, but then I realized I was lonely and missing a lot in life that could be enjoyed only with other people. Even though I was with people in my home, at work, and at church, I never really entered in, but remained aloof and detached. I participated only if I could be in control of the situation, because then I felt safe. I am sure that many of you know exactly what I am talking about.

The ability to connect with others cannot happen if one of the parties is trying to control the other. We are not created by God to be controlled; therefore, we will always resent it. Eventually people get tired of being controlled, and begin to prefer relationships where they have the freedom to be who they are and make some of the decisions that need to be made. If you have a tendency to want to control people and situations so you don't get hurt, I strongly encourage you to give it up and learn how to do relationships God's way.

As I grew in my relationship with God, He taught me that I needed to trust people and be vulnerable even though I would get hurt from time to time. He promised me that when I was hurt He would heal me and enable me to go on and try again. I have been deeply hurt from time to time by people I was in relationship with, but I refused to let it make me bitter and suspicious. Love makes allowances for the weaknesses and flaws of others. People certainly are not perfect, but in the end, they are worth the effort. Few things on earth compare to the joy and benefits of a close, connected relationship with another human being.

You can feel close to people if you will choose to open your heart to them and if you are willing to go through the difficulties we all encounter when developing good relationships. I believe that when we have a problem in a relationship but we resolve to work through it, in the end the bond is made closer than it was before. Too many people give up at the first hint of difficulty. They have resolved to never get hurt again, and that decision prevents them from the joy of close friendships and intimacy with their spouses and other family members.

I want to stress again that we cannot have closeness if we are not willing to go through some pain. People simply are not perfect, and we do make mistakes. It is the willingness to forgive and go on that makes relationships strong.

The feeling of being connected and close to others definitely goes under the heading of "Good Emotions." I knew a man who never in his life allowed himself to be close to anyone; he died lonely, and nobody misses him. That is a sad ending to a life. He missed it all and doesn't get a do-over. The Bible says that we have one opportunity to live and then comes judgment (see Heb. 9:27), so I think we should try to make the one opportunity we have count.

The Beauty of Empathy

It is wonderful to feel empathy for others who are hurting, oppressed, or being mistreated in any way. I absolutely hate to see people hurting with no one to help them. God feels compassion for and takes action to help those who are hurting, and we should too. True compassion begins with a feeling that becomes so intense it moves us to action.

One of the sweetest examples of this behavior took place at the Seattle Special Olympics in 1976. Nine young competitors, all mentally or physically disabled, assembled at the starting line for the 100-yard dash. At the sound of the gun, they all started running toward the finish line—all except one little boy, who stumbled and fell and began to cry.

One by one, the other children stopped and looked back. Then each one of them turned around, walked toward the little boy, and gathered around, comforting him. A little girl leaned down and kissed his skinned knee, saying, "This will make it better."

All nine children stood up, linked arms, and walked toward the finish line together. That day a stadium full of able-bodied spectators learned about what really makes us happy.

I believe Satan is on a mission to desensitize us to the pain other people go through. It seems that all we hear on television or read in the papers is about some terrible thing someone has done to someone else. It has become so commonplace that we can be guilty of not even paying much attention to it. Dave remembers when the first paperboy was robbed in St. Louis where we live. He said the entire city was shocked that such a thing could happen. Now, because of such extreme violence, a paperboy being robbed wouldn't even be worthy of mentioning in the news.

The Danger of Becoming Hard-Hearted

> I will give them one heart [a new heart] and I will put a
> new spirit within them; and I will take the stony [unnat-
> urally hardened] heart out of their flesh, and will give
> them a heart of flesh [sensitive and responsive to the
> touch of their God].   *(Ezekiel 11:19)*

This scripture means a lot to me because I was a hard-hearted person due to the abuse I had suffered in the earlier years of my life. This Bible verse gave me hope that I could change. God gives us things in seed form and we must work with the Holy Spirit to bring them to full maturity. This is much like the fruit of the Spirit, which is in us but needs to be watered with God's Word and developed through use.

As believers in Jesus, we have tender hearts, but we can become hard-hearted if we are not careful in this area. I find that taking the time to really think about what people are going through in their particular situations helps me to have compassion. Jesus was moved by compassion, and we should be also. Moved to pray, or help in some way.

Empathy is a beautiful emotion and thankfully one we don't have to resist!

Let's learn to resist evil emotions that poison our lives and embrace those we can enjoy and that will bring glory to God. Emotions are a gift from God; in fact, they're a large part of what makes us human. Without them, life would be dull, and we'd be like robots. Because emotions are a vulnerable part of us, Satan seeks to take advantage and make what God intended to be a good thing into an evil thing.

I like to try to imagine all the enjoyable emotions that Adam and Eve had in the garden prior to allowing sin to enter the world. I am sure it was wonderful indeed. But when they fell into sin, their emotions fell with them. Jesus has redeemed every part of us, including our emotions. It must have been wonderful to never experience guilt, fear, hatred, jealousy, or worry—to not even have to resist any of the ugly emotions we deal with today. But even though we have to resist those emotions, we can still be free from them through Jesus Christ.

God's desire is that you enjoy the life He has provided for you, and that is impossible to do unless you learn how to control your feelings instead of letting them control you.

With God's help, you can do it!

SUGGESTED READING

Why You Act the Way You Do, Tim LaHaye, Living Books, 1988.

Spirit-Controlled Temperament, Tim LaHaye, Tyndale House, 1994.

Your Personality Tree: Discover the Real You By Uncovering the Roots of Your Personality Tree, Florence Littauer, Thomas Nelson Publishers, 1989.

Personality Plus: How to Understand Others by Understanding Yourself, Florence Littauer, Revell, 1992.

The Treasure Tree: Helping Kids Understand Their Personality, Gary and Norma Smalley & John and Cindy Trent, Thomas Nelson, 1998.

Your Spiritual Personality: Using the Strengths of Your Personality to Deepen Your Relationship with God, Marita Littauer, John Wiley & Sons, 2004.

Godly Personalities: Growing Spiritually in Your Created Personality Type, Roger Deemer, Deep River Publishers, 2011.

Wired That Way: The Comprehensive Personality Plan, Dr. Marita Littauer, Regal Books e-pub, 2006.

ABOUT THE AUTHOR

JOYCE MEYER is one of the world's leading practical Bible teachers. Her TV and radio broadcast, Enjoying Everyday Life, airs on hundreds of television networks and radio stations worldwide.

Joyce has written more than 100 inspirational books. Her bestsellers include *God Is Not Mad at You*; *Making Good Habits, Breaking Bad Habits*; *Do Yourself a Favor...Forgive*; *Living Beyond Your Feelings*; *Power Thoughts*; *Battlefield of the Mind*; *Look Great, Feel Great*; *The Confident Woman*; *I Dare You*; and *Never Give Up!*

Joyce travels extensively, holding conferences throughout the year, speaking to thousands around the world.

To contact the author, write:
Joyce Meyer Ministries
P.O. Box 655
Fenton, MO 63026
or call: 1-800-727-9673; (636) 349-0303 (outside the U.S.)

Internet address: www.joycemeyer.org

*Please include your testimony or help received
from this book when you write.
Your prayer requests are welcome.*

To contact the author in Canada, please write:
Joyce Meyer Ministries Canada
P.O. Box 7700
Vancouver, BC V6B 4E2
Canada
or call: 1-800-868-1002

In Australia, please write:
Joyce Meyer Ministries
Locked Bag 77
Mansfield Delivery Centre
Queensland 4122
Australia
or call: (07) 3349 1200
from New Zealand: 0800 448 536
from Singapore: 800 6167 032

In England, please write:
Joyce Meyer Ministries
P.O. Box 1549
Windsor SL4 1GT
United Kingdom
or call: +44 (0)1753 831102

In Germany, please write:
Joyce Meyer Ministries
Postfach 761001
22060 Hamburg
Germany
or call: +49 (0)40 / 88 88 4 11 11

In India, please write:
Joyce Meyer Ministries
Nanakramguda
Hyderabad - 500 008
Andhra Pradesh
India
or call: 91-40-2300 6777

In Russia, please write:
Joyce Meyer Ministries
P.O. Box 14
Moscow 109316
Russia
or call: (095) 727-14-68

In South Africa, please write:
Joyce Meyer Ministries—South Africa
P.O. Box 5
Cape Town 8000
South Africa
or call: (27) 21-701 1056

OTHER BOOKS BY JOYCE MEYER

100 Ways to Simplify Your Life

21 Ways to Finding Peace and Happiness

Any Minute

Approval Addiction

The Battle Belongs to the Lord

Battlefield of the Mind*

Battlefield of the Mind for Kids

Battlefield of the Mind for Teens

Battlefield of the Mind Devotional

Be Anxious for Nothing*

Being the Person God Made You to Be

Beauty for Ashes

Change Your Words, Change Your Life

The Confident Mom

The Confident Woman

The Confident Woman Devotional

Do Yourself a Favor . . . Forgive

Eat the Cookie . . . Buy the Shoes

Eight Ways to Keep the Devil Under Your Feet

Ending Your Day Right

Enjoying Where You Are on the Way to Where You Are Going

The Everyday Life Bible

Filled with the Spirit

God Is Not Mad at You

Hearing from God Each Morning

How to Hear from God*

How to Succeed at Being Yourself

Start Your New Life Today
Starting Your Day Right
Straight Talk
Teenagers Are People Too!
Trusting God Day by Day
The Word, the Name, the Blood
Woman to Woman
You Can Begin Again

JOYCE MEYER SPANISH TITLES

Belleza en Lugar de Cenizas (Beauty for Ashes)
Cambia Tus Palabras, Cambia Tu Vida
(Change Your Words, Change Your Life)
Como Formar Buenos Habitos y Romper Malos Habitos
(Making Good Habits, Breaking Bad Habits)
Dios No Está Enojado Contigo (God Is Not Mad at You)
El Campo de Batalla de la Mente (Battlefield of the Mind)
Empezando Tu Día Bien (Starting Your Day Right)
Hazte un Favor a Ti Mismo…Perdona (Do Yourself a Favor…Forgive)
Madre Segura de Sí Misma (The Confident Mom)
Pensamientos de Poder (Power Thoughts)
Termina Bien Tu Día (Ending Your Day Right)
Usted Puede Comenzar de Nuevo (You Can Begin Again)

BOOKS BY DAVE MEYER

Life Lines

* *Study Guide available for this title*